2ND Edition

Community Policing

How to Get Started

Robert Trojanowicz
Bonnie Bucqueroux

anderson publishing co.
2035 Reading Road
Cincinnati, OH 45202
800-582-7295

Community Policing: How to Get Started, Second Edition

Copyright © 1994, 1998
          Anderson Publishing Co.
          2035 Reading Rd.
          Cincinnati, OH 45202

   Phone 800.582.7295 or 513.421.4142
Web Site www.andersonpublishing.com

Library of Congress Cataloging-in-Publication Data

Trojanowicz, Robert C., 1941-
    Community policing: how to get started / Robert Trojanowicz
Bonnie Bucqueroux. -- 2nd ed.
        p.   cm.
    Includes bibliographical references.
    ISBN 0-87084-877-1 (pbk.)
    1. Community policing--United States. 2. Crime prevention--United
States--Citizen participation. 3. Police-community relations--
United States. I. Bucqueroux, Bonnie. II. Title.
HV7936.C83T76   1998
363.2' 3' 0973--dc21   98-17432
                                                         CIP

Cover design by Tin Box Studio/Cincinnati, OH   EDITOR Gail Eccleston
Cover photo credit: ©1997 Jay Corbett/Photonica   ASSISTANT EDITOR Elizabeth A. Shipp
                                                   ACQUISITIONS EDITOR Michael C. Braswell

DEDICATION

This book is dedicated to all of the police administrators, upper command, supervisors, and officers who took risks with implementing and practicing community policing. You often met resistance, were ridiculed, and even forced to leave the department because of your commitment to providing community policing services to those citizens you served.

We salute you!

—These heartfelt words were written by
Bob Trojanowicz during the last year of his life.

ACKNOWLEDGMENTS

There is simply no way to thank Bob Trojanowicz for the support and opportunities he offered me. But more importantly, Bob influenced thousands of people at hundreds of police agencies for whom he offered a vision of the future where every officer could contribute to excellence.

Bob was the Ph.D. son of a beat cop father with an eighth-grade education, and he always said that it was his dad who taught him everything he knew about community policing. Bob felt that honoring his father meant devoting his life to giving line-level officers the responsibility and authority to do quality work.

It was this down-to-earth, pragmatic side, enriched by his work in the field, that allowed Bob to lead Michigan State University's School of Criminal Justice and the National Center for Community Policing to unparalleled respect within the worlds of policing and of academe. He knew that knowledge means nothing without wisdom, and that wisdom cannot change the world if no one hears or understands it. His lifelong goal was to open up the ivory tower and make it accessible and relevant to today's world – in essence, practicing the principles of community policing within the university.

His dedication to community policing reform drove him to push himself harder than he should have. There was the time that Bob, who hated to fly, was due back from Brazil late at night. He had gone to Sao Paulo a second time, in a sincere effort to help the national police force embrace community policing as a means of ending the murder of the street children, often at the hands of police. The problem wounded Bob on many levels. Of course, his primary concern was for the hundreds of youngsters killed and injured each year, but it also pained him that police officers could participate in such monstrous acts. This is the kind of work that takes a toll beyond the hours and the physical and mental effort.

I had expected – and hoped – that Bob might slow down a bit and take a breather to recover after such an exhausting trip. Yet there he was, back on the job early the next morning, on almost no sleep. When I asked why he didn't pace himself a bit more – after all, we want to be in this for the long haul – he would say, "But they need the help now."

Bob lived long enough to see his ideas take root, but sadly, his sudden death in 1994 robbed him of the chance to see community policing bloom. Indeed all who knew him wish that he was still here to clear away the dead branches and perhaps do a little pruning. Community policing remains a living and breathing entity, and Bob's many disciples will be the generation that shapes it in their communities. And we will all remember Bob's motto, "Until we are all safe, no one is truly safe."

More Thanks

I would also like to take this opportunity to give personal and professional thanks to colleagues who have helped me in my attempts to carry on. In particular, I want to thank my friend Drew Diamond of the Police Executive Research Forum, who burns with the same messianic dedication. Thanks as well to Bill Matthews of the Community Policing Consortium, who informs the process with the special fervor that he brings from his work in public housing. Thanks also to Ira Harris and James McIver of the National Organization of Black Law Enforcement Executives for their sincere commitment to building community partnerships.

Thanks and best wishes to Leroy O'Shield, the chief of police for the Chicago Housing Authority and a "Trojo" disciple always willing to try new ideas. Heartfelt appreciation also to Harry Dolan, an extraordinarily talented chief in Grand Rapids, Michigan, who shared Bob's distaste for elitism. Bruce Benson, director of Michigan State University Department of Police and Public Safety, continues to implement Bob's vision. Special thanks as well to Chief Ron Sloan of Arvada, Colorado, another of the "Trojo" circle, many of whom are now taking their rightful place in positions of power.

Personal thanks to Bob's good friends John Henry Campbell, retired dean of the FBI Academy, and Robert Ressler, retired FBI profiler, for their continued support.

Within academe, Dr. Carl Taylor at Michigan State University honors Bob's memory with his work on community violence, and he carries on Bob's vision of building strong neighborhoods through his Center for Community Leadership. Thanks to Frank Ochberg, M.D., not only for his personal support of me and my efforts, but for his continuing commitment to the Critical Incident Analysis Group concept, which he co-founded with Bob Trojanowicz. This is the multi-disciplinary group that attempts to bring the knowledge of the university to bear on current events that shape our lives, such as building the FBI/Militia Hotline to facilitate communication with the goal of saving lives.

Special thanks to Bruce Shapiro, author of *One Violent Crime* (Harper Collins, 1998), for the exceptional intelligence and insight that he brings to our understanding of the dynamics of violence and the system's ability to address its many forms.

Stan Soffin, Bill Coté, and Sue Carter have sustained and nurtured me in my new home at Michigan State University's School of Journalism, with the Victims and the Media Program.

Personal Thanks

This book could not have been done without the unwavering support of my amazing husband Drew Howard, particularly during these last few years of loss. Sister Tina (the best sister in the world) did her best to keep me healthy along the way, while her husband (and my friend) Dave kept my computer humming. And my warmest thanks to my mother, Helen McLanus, for her independence and her continued personal growth – she serves as an example to us all.

* * *

In remembrance of my stepdaughter Kim, who taught me that no matter how hard you try, you cannot save them all (http://members.aol.com/bucqui/kimmy).

Bonnie Bucqueroux

PREFACE

This book has been revised and reorganized to reflect changing needs and new questions in the field. It remains impossible to give a standardized list of rules that police agencies should follow to implement community policing. Instead, we present questions that can help each police agency find the right answers for them.

The book opens with the Community Policing Implementation Checklist, which can be used to organize, create, monitor, and evaluate the process. The succeeding chapters offer information and ideas that help to inform the questions on the list.

INTRODUCTION

The first edition of this book and Trojanowicz and Bucqueroux's first book on community policing (*Community Policing: A Contemporary Perspective*) had the immediate effect of putting into focus the idea that the world of policing is improvable. In setting forth the philosophy of community policing and the underlying principles, the authors, Professor Robert Trojanowicz and Bonnie Bucqueroux, melded the best of policing traditions with contemporary practices. At the same time, they identified serious gaps in police service and showed how the implementation of community policing closes those gaps.

With the publication of this second edition comes the realization of how much policing has changed and how much it has remained the same. Steady progress has been made in understanding and accepting the principles of community policing. The language of community engagement and problem solving has taken hold in everything from department mission statements to recruit training curricula. The U.S. Department of Justice extended its existing support for community policing with the creation of the Office of Community Oriented Policing Services (COPS) and funding for the training of community policing officers from more than 9,000 police and sheriffs departments. The development of Regional Community Policing Institutes throughout the country is underway. Police officers in every jurisdiction in the nation are engaging in collaborative problem-solving partnerships with their communities at unprecedented levels.

In the face of these and other positive changes, much remains the same. Among police, there still exists a strong and sometimes desperate resistance to change. Many police officers and police executives have learned to "talk the talk" of community policing but will not "walk the walk." Some police agencies still cling to their authoritarian organizational structure. This structure, along with the leadership supporting it, is stifling the creativity of police officers, dampening their initiative, and shutting out community partnerships. With the passing of Robert Trojanowicz, we lost one of those rare individuals who was willing to walk the walk of change.

Bob Trojanowicz believed in the dedication and skill of police officers and in the commitment of communities to work with their police to improve the quality of life for everybody. Throughout his life, he worked tirelessly with police officers, communities, government agencies, and universities to implement positive changes in police service. As the director of Michigan State University's School of Criminal Justice and the National Center for Community Policing (which Bob founded), and as a Research Fellow in the Kennedy School of Government Criminal Justice Policy and Management Program at Harvard University, "Trojo" instructed, assisted, and influenced this generation of police officers and set the tone of community policing for the next generation.

Community policing is policing at its best. This book, with its updated information, will continue to guide those who are interested in creating and maintaining safer communities through the understanding of the community policing philosophy and the implementation of its practices.

Drew Diamond
Senior Researcher
Police Executive Research Forum

TABLE OF CONTENTS

SECTION I
What Is Community Policing?

SECTION II
The Planning Process:
A Community Policing Approach to Change

SECTION III
A Formula for Success
Community Policing = LEADERSHIP (Community Building + Problem Solving)

SECTION IV
Building Partnerships with the Community

SECTION V
Issues in Hiring and Training

SECTION VI
Management, Supervision, Program Assessment, Performance Evaluation, and Promotion

SECTION VII
The Future of Community Policing

Community Policing Implementation Checklist

Vision/Values/Mission

☐ Has the organization written or revised these statements to reflect an organization-wide commitment to the philosophy and principles of community policing?

☐ Does the process include soliciting input from all levels of the police department, including sworn, non-sworn, and civilian personnel?

☐ Does the process include soliciting input from outside the police department: the community, businesses, civic officials, public agencies, community institutions (schools, hospitals, the faith community), non-profit agencies, formal and informal community leaders, and community residents?

Code of Ethics

☐ Has the organization written or revised a *Code of Ethics* that reflects the principles of community policing?

☐ Does producing a new *Code of Ethics* encourage input from inside and outside the organization?

☐ Does the *Code of Ethics* discuss issues such as civility, courtesy, respect for civil rights (including the right to privacy), and sensitivity to diversity?

Leadership & Management Style

☐ Does the department support and exhibit leadership at all levels in implementing, institutionalizing, and maintaining the momentum of community policing? Does the department empower the community to support and exhibit leadership in this regard?

☐ Does the implementation plan reflect inverting the power pyramid, shifting power, authority, and responsibility to line-level personnel?

❑ Do managers serve as *facilitators* who access resources from inside and outside the department in service of community building and problem solving?

❑ Do managers act as *models* for the behavior that they want others to follow? Does this include demonstrating sensitivity to diversity?

❑ Do managers act as *coaches* who inspire and instruct?

❑ Do managers act as *mentors* who guide and support?

❑ Does the internal management style exhibit a striving for collaboration and consensus?

❑ Does the department have a mechanism to prevent, identify, and deal with burnout?

Role of Chief Executive Officers (CEOs)

❑ How does the CEO exhibit leadership internally and externally for the commitment to and changes required by implementing community policing?

❑ Does the CEO understand and accept the depth of change and the time required to implement community policing, as framed by the principles of community policing?

❑ Does the CEO practice the philosophy of community policing by collaborating with others in the department?

❑ Has the CEO succeeded in assembling and educating a management team committed to translating the new vision into action?

❑ Is the CEO a consistent internal and external advocate for community policing? Is he or she ready with the definition and success stories for any group or occasion?

❑ How does the CEO express commitment to risk-taking within the organization?

❑ What kinds of leadership does the CEO provide in support of community building and community-based problem solving?

❑ How will the CEO deal with the internal resistance/backlash, particularly from middle managers, first-line supervisors, and others who perceive community policing as a rejection of the prevailing police culture?

❑ How can the CEO cut red tape and remove bureaucratic obstacles that stifle creativity?

❑ How does the CEO express openness to new ideas from all levels of the organization, including line-level personnel?

❑ Does the CEO back those who make well-intentioned mistakes?

❑ Does the CEO jump the chain of command on occasion to reinforce the commitment to community policing within the organization?

❑ How has the CEO committed the organization to deal with the small percentage of "bad apples" whose actions can undermine the trust of the community?

❑ How will the CEO deal with marginal employees who are unwilling or unable to translate the community policing practice into the hard and risky work of effecting real change?

Role of Top Command

❑ How does top command exhibit leadership internally and externally for the commitment to and changes required by implementing community policing?

❑ How does top command express the philosophy and the Ten Principles in their work?

❑ How will they translate the vision into practice? How will that planning process model community building and problem solving internally?

❑ How will top command plan for dealing with the internal resistance?

❑ Does top command cut red tape and remove bureaucratic obstacles that stifle creativity?

❑ How does top command create a structure to allow new ideas from all levels of the organization, including line-level personnel, to surface to the top?

❑ Does top command back those who make well-intentioned mistakes?

❑ Does top command jump the chain of command on occasion to reinforce the commitment to community policing within the organization?

❑ How has top command operationalized and institutionalized zero-tolerance for abuse of authority and excessive force?

❑ How does top command deal with marginal employees who are unwilling or unable to translate the community policing practice into the hard and risky work of effecting real change?

Role of Middle Managers & First-Line Supervisors

❑ How do middle managers and first-line supervisors exhibit leadership internally and externally for the commitment to and changes required by implementing community policing?

❑ How do middle managers and first-line supervisors express the philosophy and the Ten Principles in their work?

❑ How are middle managers and first-line supervisors authorized and encouraged to provide line-level personnel sufficient freedom and autonomy to engage in community building and creative, community-based problem solving?

❑ How do middle managers and first-line supervisors express their roles as facilitators, models, coaches, and mentors?

❑ How does the organization support middle managers and first-line supervisors who take risks?

❑ Are middle managers and first-line supervisors authorized and encouraged to spend more time in the community, supervising line-level personnel, and supporting community building and community-based problem solving?

❑ Has the organization been streamlined to allow middle managers and first-line supervisors to solicit the resources required to support community building and community-based problem solving?

Role of Line Officers

❑ How do line officers exhibit leadership internally and externally for the commitment to and changes required by implementing community policing?

❑ How do line officers express the philosophy and the Ten Principles in their work?

❑ Do line-level officers engage in community building and problem solving in their work? Are they given the freedom, autonomy, and opportunity to do so?

❑ Do line-level officers receive support from management in carrying out their commitment to community policing?

❑ How do ideas from line-level officers move upward within the organization?

❑ Has the job really changed?

Role of Non-Sworn & Civilian Personnel

❑ How do non-sworn and civilian personnel exhibit leadership internally and externally for the commitment to and changes required by implementing community policing?

❑ How do non-sworn and civilian personnel express the philosophy and the Ten Principles in their work?

❑ Do non-sworn and civilian personnel engage in community building and problem solving within the scope of their work? Are they given the freedom, autonomy, and opportunity to do so?

❑ Do non-sworn and civilian personnel receive support from management in carrying out their commitment to community policing?

❑ How do ideas from non-sworn and civilian personnel move upward within the organization?

❑ Has the job really changed?

Information Management

❑ Does the organization have systems to collect, analyze, and share relevant information on problems in the community internally (among all levels of the organization, including sworn, non-sworn, and civilian personnel) and externally (with the broader community)?

❑ Does the organization gather and analyze information on social and physical disorder and quality-of-life concerns in addition to crime data? Is the information analyzed in terms of geographic area?

❑ Are data and analyses provided in their most useful forms?

❑ Are there formal and informal opportunities for information gathered at the line level to surface to the top within the organization? Is there a two-way flow of information?

❑ Are there formal and informal opportunities for officers assigned permanently in beats to share information with other patrol officers who patrol the same areas? Are such opportunities encouraged at all levels?

❑ Has the organization developed a means of capturing and documenting (tracking) problems solved in neighborhood areas including solutions that do not involve arrest?

❑ Does the management style support exhibiting greater sensitivity to issues of diversity within the department?

❑ Is the department taking full advantage of new technologies, such as the Internet and the World Wide Web, to interact with the community?

Planning/Program Evaluation

❑ Has the organization devoted sufficient time and resources to make the most of strategic planning to implement community policing?

❑ What mechanisms are employed to solicit input from inside and outside the organization to ensure input from line-level police personnel and community residents?

❑ Does the strategic planning process itself provide opportunities to begin building new partnerships?

❑ Does the strategic planning process itself provide opportunities to empower line-level personnel?

❑ As a "reality check," can the participants involved in planning clearly describe what the plan is designed to achieve?

❑ How does the organization inject objectivity into the process, as a guarantee that the tough questions will be asked?

❑ Does the monitoring process include capturing qualitative as well as quantitative outcomes?

❑ Can the planning/program evaluation staff cross organizational lines and coordinate directly with management information system staff?

❑ Have program assessments changed to reflect the many different kinds of success, such as overall harm reduction?

❑ Is there a plan to keep modifying and "tweaking" the implementation plan? Is there a strategy to stay abreast of new opportunities and new problems?

Resources/Finances

❑ Has the department realistically analyzed its resource needs to implement community policing? Has the police agency clearly justified the need for additional resources?

❑ Are residents of the jurisdiction willing to pay more in taxes to obtain community policing?

❑ Has the police department fully explored local, state, and federal grants available for community policing?

❑ Has the police department fully explored private sources of funding (businesses, foundations, etc.)?

❑ Has the police department restructured and prioritized workload and services to free up patrol time for community policing? Has the department worked with the community on developing alternatives to traditional handling of calls for service?

❑ Has the police organization considered flattening the management hierarchy as a means of creating more patrol positions for community policing?

❑ Has the police organization considered despecializing (eliminating, reducing, or restructuring specialized units) as a means of creating more patrol positions for community policing?

❑ Has the police organization made the best possible use of civilians and volunteers as a means of freeing up patrol officer time for community policing?

❑ What mode of transportation is the best for officers doing community policing in different areas with different needs (e.g., patrol cars, scooters, bicycles, etc.)?

❑ Are officers outfitted with appropriate technology (e.g., cellular phones, pagers, answering machines/voice mail, fax machines, laptop/notebook computers, access to computer network, etc.)?

❑ Do neighborhood-based officers require office space? Is free space available? What about furniture? What about utilities?

Recruiting

❑ Has the organization considered expanding its recruiting efforts to reach college students in nontraditional fields, such as education and social work, to educate them about how community policing might provide an appealing alternative?

❑ Has the organization succeeded in finding ways to attract women and minorities?

❑ Does recruiting literature explain the new demands required by a community policing approach? Does it also discuss job satisfaction?

Selection & Hiring

❑ Has the organization conducted a job-task analysis of the new "community policing" entry-level officer position, and has it developed a new job description?

❑ Do individuals and groups inside and outside the department have opportunities for input in developing criteria for the selection process?

❑ Do selection criteria emphasize verbal and written communication skills, the ability to work closely with people from all walks of life, and interest in developing skills in conflict resolution and creative problem solving?

❑ Do civil service requirements reflect the principles of community policing?

❑ Are candidates directly informed about the expectations of officers involved in community policing?

❑ Is the screening process designed to weed out those who categorically reject the principles of community policing?

Training

❑ Do plans include the eventual training of everyone in the department, sworn, non-sworn, and civilian, in the philosophy, practice, and principles of community policing?

❑ Do plans include building community policing into all training opportunities: recruit, field training, in-service, roll call, and management?

❑ Has the organization recently conducted a comprehensive training skills needs assessment to determine the actual knowledge, skills, and abilities needed to perform community policing as an officer?

❑ Does the organization provide new and existing line-level personnel sufficient skills training in communication, interpersonal relationships, conflict resolution, problem solving, and sensitivity to diversity?

❑ Do field training officers "practice" the principles of community policing so that recruits see how they are implemented?

❑ Are middle managers and first-line supervisors trained concerning how their role changes in a community policing organization?

❑ Is there a system in place to capture suggestions and recommendations on training from individuals and groups inside and outside the department?

❑ Has the organization considered bringing culturally representative residents in to recruit training to work with recruits on "real life" problem-solving exercises?

❑ Does the department maintain a library of information on a wide range of topics that can broaden experience and understanding? Does the department provide opportunities for further learning through the Internet and the World Wide Web?

Performance Evaluation

❑ Are performance evaluations based on job descriptions that reflect the principles of community policing and that emphasize taking action to make a positive difference in the community as the yardstick for success?

❑ Did the process of developing performance evaluations reflect broad input from inside and outside the organization?

❑ Are performance evaluations written from the citizen's point of view (the public who are the recipients of police service), rather than to serve the organization's bureaucratic needs?

❑ Do performance evaluations encourage risk-taking, by avoiding penalties for well-intentioned mistakes and by rewarding creativity?

❑ Do performance evaluations for managers and supervisors reflect the shift from "controller" to "facilitator," as well as the roles of model, coach, and mentor?

❑ Do performance evaluations for managers and supervisors reward efforts to delegate not only responsibility but authority?

❑ Do performance evaluations for managers and supervisors reward them for cutting red tape and removing bureaucratic obstacles that can stifle creativity?

❑ Do performance evaluations for managers and supervisors reward their efforts to secure resources for community building and community-based problem solving?

❑ Do performance evaluations for managers and supervisors reward them for developing collaborative partnerships with individuals and groups outside the organization?

❑ Do performance evaluations for managers and supervisors reward them for efforts to generate internal support for community policing?

❑ Do performance evaluations for managers and supervisors reward actions taken to reduce internal friction/backlash?

❑ Do performance evaluations for special units (e.g., detectives, traffic officers) reward members for initiating, participating in, and/or supporting community policing, specifically community building and community-based problem solving?

❑ Do performance evaluations for non-sworn and civilian personnel reward them for initiating, participating in, and/or supporting community policing, specifically community building and community-based problem solving?

❑ Do performance evaluations for patrol officers reward them for using their free patrol time to initiate community building and community-based problem solving?

❑ Do performance evaluations for officers reward meeting the special needs of specific groups – women, the elderly, minorities, juveniles?

❑ Do performance evaluations for officers reward sensitivity to diversity?

❑ Do performance evaluations for officers reward developing and strengthening collaborative partnerships?

❑ Does the performance evaluation process allow the community opportunities for formal and informal input into the assessment?

❑ Do performance evaluations for officers reward them for initiating and maintaining community building and community-based problem solving initiatives? Creativity? Innovation? Risk-taking? Preventing problems?

❑ Do performance evaluations for officers gauge success on whether their efforts attempted to improve life in the community?

Promotions

❑ Did the development of promotional criteria include broad input from inside and outside the organization?

❑ Do promotional criteria reflect qualitative and well as quantitative measures?

❑ Do promotional exams, interviews, and oral boards require candidates to express their knowledge of and support for the philosophy and principles of community policing?

❑ Do civil service requirements reflect the philosophy and principles of community policing?

❑ Does the process allow one or more representatives from the community to sit on oral board panels?

❑ Does the promotional process result in managers and supervisors able and eager to make the transition from the "controller" to "facilitator" model? Does it produce managers who act as models, coaches, and facilitators?

❑ Do officers who work directly in the community receive credit in the promotional process for the skills and expertise acquired by serving in this capacity?

❑ Does the promotional process recognize that a well-intentioned failure or mistake should not necessarily be perceived as a minus – just as a clean slate is not necessarily a plus if it is indicative of a rote and perfunctory performance?

❑ Are the right people being promoted?

Honors/Awards

❑ Does the formal and informal honors and awards process allow those who do an extraordinary job of community-based problem solving to be recognized for their efforts?

Discipline

❏ Has the organization adopted a determined leadership approach toward those whose behavior has the potential to undermine community policing?

❏ Does the organization provide formal and informal support for "whistle-blowers" on this issue?

❏ Does the organization reject the excuse that trivial infractions do not warrant the time expended on paperwork required to enforce discipline?

❏ Is the community a partner in accountability?

❏ Has the department adopted a zero-tolerance approach to abuse of authority and use of excessive force?

Unions

❏ Are unions directly and immediately involved as partners in the planning process to implement community policing?

❏ How does the police organization plan to educate union representatives about the need to change some terms in the contract to implement community policing (e.g., providing officers greater autonomy and flexibility, assigning officers to permanent beats and work hours)?

❏ Should the union address the issue of whether community policing is implemented as a change for all patrol officers or as a specialized assignment?

Structuring the Delivery of Patrol Services

❏ Does the police organization prioritize calls to free up patrol time for community building and community-based problem solving by all patrol officers?

❏ Has the department involved the community in decisions about prioritizing calls for service? Are call takers and dispatchers trained with an acceptable protocol to explain to callers why they may have to wait for a response to a non-emergency call or have their call handled by an alternative? Are communications personnel trained to use discretion in these situations?

❏ How do various levels of the police organization address the need to educate the public about the rationale for prioritizing calls as a means of enhancing opportunities for community building and problem solving?

❏ Does the police organization have a range of alternatives ready to handle non-emergency calls for service to relieve officers of the responsibility?

Beat Boundaries & Assignments
(where applicable for community policing officers and teams)

❑ Do beat boundaries correspond to neighborhood boundaries?

❑ Do other city services recognize the police beat boundaries?

❑ Considering the severity of the problems in the area, is the size of the beat manageable?

❑ Are patrol officers/teams assigned to a specific area long enough to make a difference?

❑ Does the police organization have a policy to reduce or eliminate cross-beat dispatching? Are dispatchers adhering to the policy?

❑ Are patrol officers assigned to beats assured that they will not be used to substitute whenever temporary or permanent vacancies occur elsewhere in the organization?

❑ Does the organization avoid pulling these officers for special duty – parades, special events, etc.?

❑ Are patrol officers/teams assigned to permanent shifts long enough to make a difference?

❑ Do work rules permit officers to change their hours of work as needed with a minimum of, or no, red tape?

❑ Do officers/teams assigned to beats have the same opportunities to receive overtime for appropriate activities, such as attending important evening community meetings, as other patrol counterparts do for activities considered essential to effectiveness in their job?

❑ Has the organization clarified and documented that working unpaid overtime hours in the community is appreciated, but that such dedication is not a requirement of the job nor is it considered in the performance review and promotional process?

❑ Does the assignment process ensure that such duty is not used as punishment or as a "dumping ground" for problem officers?

❑ How has the department addressed the perception that this is "special duty" with special perquisites? What strategies are used to reduce internal dissent?

Integration into Other Systems

❑ Has the department considered ways of integrating its efforts with other elements of the criminal justice system – prosecutors, courts, corrections, and probation and parole? Has the department explored opportunities to work toward a community criminal justice system?

❑ Has the department considered ways of integrating its efforts with other agencies that deliver public services – social services, public health, mental health, code enforcement? Has the department explored opportunities to work toward community-oriented public service?

❑ Are the police and the community prepared to serve as the catalyst to integrate community criminal justice and community-oriented public service into a total community approach?

❑ Has the department explored strategies such as the Neighborhood Network Center concept as a means of encouraging a total community approach?

❑ Is the department planning to take full advantage of new technology, including the Internet and World Wide Web, as a means of interacting with the community?

SECTION I
What Is Community Policing?

Community Policing at the Crossroads

Community policing clearly has the potential to become the definitive approach that all police agencies will follow in the twenty-first century. It has exploded from the early days of promising experiments in a handful of cities to the nationwide movement of today. That phenomenal growth stands as a testament to the power behind the idea of encouraging people and their police to forge new partnerships to address the issues of crime, fear of crime, and disorder in their communities.

At the same time, the movement also faces enormous challenges in fulfilling its potential, in large part because of its success. As we will see, the danger in the "bandwagon effect" often means that people jump on board without a full appreciation of what community policing is and without the know-how to make it work.

At one extreme are those police agencies that push change so quickly and broadly that the backlash overwhelms good intentions. On the other end of that spectrum are cases where timidity, misunderstanding, or inertia cause police departments to adopt the rhetoric of community policing without making any substantive change. Others simply re-define community policing to cover the status quo.

As a result, the biggest challenge facing community policing may well be that it has been stretched to cover so many different definitions, ideas, and activities that it is in danger of becoming a meaningless buzzword.

A Brief History

If community policing is to fulfill its potential, maybe it is time to revisit its roots, as a way of deepening our understanding of what those two words are meant to convey. Community policing emerged from frustrations with business as usual and a growing recognition that many of the problems associated with so-called "modern" and "scientific" policing might well stem from the realization that it had inadvertently severed the ties between people and their police. By the 1950s and early 1960s, the face of policing had become the clear-eyed professionals of the Los Angeles Police Department on TV's "Dragnet." A far cry from the boisterous, ill-educated, and untrained beat cop of old, Jack Webb's portrayal of Sgt. Joe Friday offered us the image of the cool professional who uses intellect instead of muscle.

The advent of modern communications and mass transportation transformed policing, pulling beat cops out of their neighborhoods into patrol cars dispatched from central headquarters in response to calls from those new-fangled telephones. The logic was simple: a call comes in, a patrol car is dispatched, and officers trained as crime fighters arrest the bad guys. In between calls for service, random patrol serves as a visible deterrent to crime.

What could be more sensible and more democratic? The few bad guys who succeed in getting away will eventually be found by steely-eyed investigators like Joe Friday and his partner. The mission was clear: arresting the bad guys is the key to making the community safe, and a grateful public will therefore gladly provide police any information and assistance they need, which is basically limited to "just the facts, ma'am" and paying taxes.

Yet something in that reactive method of policing went terribly awry. An early indicator of problems to come with the traditional police approach was the infamous Kitty Genovese case in New York City in 1964. Genovese was mugged, then stabbed and beaten to death in the courtyard of her apartment complex. Although 38 of her neighbors heard her screams for approximately one-half hour, none of them came to her aid or called the police. Former *New York Times* Managing Editor Abe Rosenthal, who was then a young reporter, interviewed the residents, asking why no one called police. Most said that they "didn't want to get involved" or that they didn't know or trust the police. This case highlighted growing concern that, particularly in urban areas, the sense of community and concern for one's neighbors had eroded and that people were becoming estranged from their police.

Then, between 1965 and 1970, violent crime surged dramatically, adding to the sense that society was careening out of control. Although some of the increase was attributable to new and improved reporting, nevertheless between 1965 and 1970, murder rates jumped 55 percent; aggravated assault, 48 percent; and robbery, 124 percent.[1] There is no precise way to measure the escalation in fear, but remember that this eruption of violent crime occurred against a backdrop of anti-war protests on college campuses and riots in our major cities. What had gone wrong? And how did the police fall from grace so abruptly that young people were now branding them as *pigs*?

Thoughtful practitioners in the field and concerned academics began to look at how modern methods and new technologies had disrupted the traditional relationship between people and police. The old-fashioned beat cop may not have had much education or training, but he knew the community and the people in it; indeed, he was one of them. That beat cop served as the department's liaison and ombudsman to the neighborhood, and in exchange for that decentralized and personalized service, people served as the officer's eyes and ears. The transition to so-called professional policing emphasized efficiency at the expense of a daily, face-to-face relationship.

By the late 1970s and early 1980s, a handful of experiments were launched to see whether it was possible to re-invent the old-fashioned beat cop for the modern era. The C.S. Mott Foundation of Flint, Michigan, invested millions of dollars in implementing foot patrol citywide. The initiative was evaluated by the late Dr. Robert Trojanowicz, who was then a Professor at Michigan State University's School of Criminal Justice. Under Trojanowicz' tutelage, the Flint officers were trained to become community-based problem solvers, collaborating with formal and informal community leaders and average citizens. At the same time, Professor George Kelling of Northeastern University was monitoring The Police Foundation foot-patrol initiative in Newark, New Jersey. In this case, the officers were not given special training.

Though not conclusive, the results of both experiments strongly suggested that there was a special synergy created when the police and the community worked together, building a sense of community and solving problems. As Kelling said, "We began to realize that we were groping our way toward something new and powerful."

In 1982, Kelling and James Q. Wilson co-authored a ground-breaking article titled "Broken Windows"[2] that appeared in the *Atlantic Monthly* magazine. The story explored the role that disorder plays in setting the stage for crime. The authors noted that, even in affluent neighborhoods, if you leave one broken window in a building unrepaired, people inevitably break others. As researcher Wesley Skogan noted, the biggest predictor of crime and drug problems in any given neighborhood is whether it appears to be on its way up – or down.[3] Part of that "groping" toward a new way of policing therefore included encouraging police to focus on so-called "quality of life" issues as a means of inoculating communities against serious crime.

Professor Herman Goldstein of the University of Wisconsin initiated the concept of problem-oriented policing with its framework of the SARA model, which challenges police to explore the dynamics and the context that allows chronic crime problems to persist, as a means of crafting comprehensive and creative solutions.

Decentralizing and personalizing police service through strategies such as foot patrol not only addressed crime but also fear of crime, which can be as serious a problem as crime itself, since it keeps law-abiding citizens imprisoned in their own homes. Those early foot-patrol experiments showed that people were able to overcome their fears and join police in proactive initiatives if they could count on an officer as "theirs." Instead of asking a faceless bureaucracy filled with strangers for help, people gained confidence from knowing that there was an officer in their neighborhood on whom they could rely.

Settling on a New Name

As the concept began to take shape, it became obvious that the term "foot patrol" was limiting and misleading. One unfortunate additional side effect was that it saddled this burgeoning new movement with the negative image of the old-fashioned foot patrol officer as corrupted by his or her close association with the community. Proponents of this new reform often felt that they were wasting precious energy refuting stereotypes of the past that had no relationship to today. The term *foot patrol* was also a misnomer because it referred to only one tactic that helped to promote partnerships between the police and the community. The issue was not the mode of locomotion, but how the officers explored new ways to make the areas they "owned" become safer.

By the early 1980s, a number of new names had appeared: Neighborhood-Oriented Policing, Community-Oriented Policing, Community Policing. Over time, the simplest term prevailed, and community policing was born.

True Believers

A handful of progressive and visionary police executives attempted to implement these concepts in experimental beats and ultimately as department-wide and citywide initiatives. Lee Brown, now mayor of Houston, who became chief in Atlanta and then Houston before becoming police commissioner of New York City under Mayor David Dinkins, is bringing national attention to the power of this new movement. Brown's background in academe meant that he understood the virtues in documenting and evaluating these new efforts.

Drew Diamond, now a senior researcher with the Police Executive Research Forum, used his position as chief in Tulsa, Oklahoma, to implement community policing as a full-fledged, department-wide reform. Diamond understood the power of collaboration with the community, and he forged new partnerships at all levels. His visionary work in making public housing safer remains as cutting edge today as it was then. Other reformers such as Joseph Brann in Hayward, California [and now director of the U.S. Department of Justice's Office of Community Oriented Police Services (COPS)]; Leroy O'Shield, Chicago Housing Authority; Nicholas Pastore in New Haven, Connecticut; Ron Sloan in Arvada, Colorado; Bruce Benson at Michigan State University; Betsy Watson in Texas; Robert Wadman, in various cities; and Charles Moose in Portland contributed to the community policing movement in the United States, while such visionaries as Robert Lunney and Chris Braiden did the same in Canada.

Toward a Working Definition

By the dawn of the 1990s, it was clear that community policing was more than just a tactic, strategy, or technique. This new approach had just begun to prove itself when the invention of crack cocaine in the mid-1980s brought the drug within reach of the young and the poor, thereby producing a firestorm of drug-related violence in our cities. The explosion of open-air drug markets exposed the limitations of police reliance on rapid response and arrest as the primary tools of enforcement. All too often, sweeps and crackdowns barely interrupted the drug trade on the streets, while clogging the rest of the criminal justice system to little effect. Community policing's ability to address the underlying dynamics of the problem from many directions began to demonstrate concretely that this new approach could deliver.

A full-fledged reform movement, community policing offered a new philosophy of policing based on building an equal partnership with the community. Community policing changes the paradigm from one in which the police are the experts to a model in which the police and the community work together to identify, prioritize, and solve problems that affect the quality of life in the community. By the time of the passage of the Crime Bill of 1994, it was clear that investing in this new approach to policing offered the opportunity to make a serious impact on the levels of violence in the community.

As we move toward a new century, community policing moves policing away from a narrow focus on the "bad guys" toward the recognition that harnessing the power of the law-abiding citizens in the neighborhood is the key to long-term change. While the police must always maintain the ability to react swiftly and effectively to immediate threats, community policing proposes that rapid response is only the beginning. The police must exhibit leadership in service of two goals: *community building* and *community-based problem solving*.

- **Community Building** – The police must constantly revisit ways to engage and empower the community, since ultimately it is the community itself that is responsible for its own safety. The role of the police is to help communities build the capacity to deal with their own problems.

- **Community-Based Problem Solving** – This new partnership of police and community provides opportunities to collaborate on solving the myriad of problems that communities face, including crime, drugs, fear of crime, and disorder. As we grow in our understanding of the dynamics that allow such problems to flourish, we see new opportunities to intervene in creative ways. The drug deal that goes down on the corner, for example, is the result of a complex set of factors that offer opportunities for positive intervention – a lack of recreational and job opportunities for young people; lax enforcement of curfews; poor streetlighting that allows for secrecy; lack of community involvement. The police can be the catalyst for community collaboration aimed at the pressure points that allow problems to persist.

A Basic Definition

In this media age, even the most complex issues risk being reduced to 10-second sound bites on the evening news. The reality, of course, is that community policing is far too important and far-reaching a concept to fit into the format of "25 words or less." Yet a failure to provide simple and concise definitions risks having others (who do not understand the concept) write them for you. Thus, the following is a basic definition of community policing:

> Community policing is a philosophy and an organizational strategy that promotes a new partnership between people and their police. It is based on the premise that both the police and the community must work together as equal partners to identify, prioritize, and solve contemporary problems such as crime, drugs, fear of crime, social and physical disorder, and overall neighborhood decay, with the goal of improving the overall quality of life in the area.

> Community policing requires a department-wide commitment from everyone; sworn, non-sworn, and civilian, to the community policing philosophy. It challenges all personnel to find ways to express this new philosophy in their jobs, thereby balancing the need to maintain an immediate and effective police response to individual crime incidents and emergencies with the goal of exploring new proactive initiatives aimed at solving problems before they occur or escalate.

> Community policing rests on decentralizing and personalizing police service, so that line officers have the opportunity, freedom, and mandate to focus on community building and community-based problem solving, so that each and every neighborhood can become a better and safer place in which to live and work.

The Community Policing Officer

The definition above previously included specific reference to the community policing officer (CPO) as the embodiment of the community policing philosophy. Yet, to understand the issues at stake, discussion of this controversial topic requires further discussion.

At the time of his death in 1994, Bob Trojanowicz' concept of the role of the CPO had evolved to include the hope that community policing would eventually outgrow the need to identify a specific job category as being labeled "specialist" in community policing. He understood the inherent danger in creating a split force. Trojanowicz favored abandoning specialties to free up more officers for "generalist" duty in the community, where they ~ould engage directly in community building and community-based problem ~ing. He applauded departments willing to experiment with streamlining ~tegories and flattening the hierarchy as a means of putting more offi- ~rs into neighborhoods as CPOs. He insisted that nothing could outperform a dedicated person who is given the time, opportunity, and encouragement to enlist others in developing creative initiatives designed to make neighborhoods safer.

However, Trojanowicz also understood the downside of singling out some line officers as CPOs. One problem is that other officers use their mere existence to argue that community building and problem solving are the responsibility of the CPOs – not something that *real* police do. There is also the complicated issue of determining and choosing which neighborhoods require the full-time services of a CPO – whether it is only necessary for the poor, high-crime neighborhoods, or whether it should be expanded to include other socioeconomic communities.

The hope was that CPOs would eventually succeed in putting themselves out of business, as communities empower themselves enough to shoulder the burden without needing the full-time services of an officer. The best estimate, however, was that it would take at least one dozen years for the most dangerous neighborhoods to stabilize to the point where they would not benefit from having an officer stationed there full-time.

Yet the fact remains that employing a CPO strategy, at least in "hot spot" neighborhoods, is such a potent and powerful tool that it should not be summarily dismissed or ignored merely because certain problems associated with CPOs are inevitable. Indeed, shying away from the use of CPOs to avoid internal dissent simply empowers the naysayers. Resistance is a normal consequence of change, and police managers can plan to address those frictions up front. Chief Harry Dolan of Lumberton, North Carolina, insists that the chief bears the ultimate responsibility of dealing with internal resistance. "Leadership means setting the tone that this is the way we will do business from now on," says Dolan. "And those who do not agree should understand that they will not be happy here and maybe they should think about another line of work."

The Big Six

The Big Six refers to the six groups that must be identified and must work together to ensure the success of any community policing efforts.

- **The Police Department** – Includes all personnel, from the chief to the line officer, sworn, non-sworn, and civilian.

- **The Community** – Includes everyone from formal and informal community leaders such as presidents of civic groups, ministers, and educators, to community organizers and activists, to average citizens.

- **Elected Civic Officials** – Includes the mayor, city manager, city council, and any county, state, and federal officials whose support can affect community policing's future.

- **The Business Community** – Includes the full range of businesses, from major corporations to the mom-and-pop store on the corner.

- **Other Agencies** – Includes public agencies (code enforcement, social services, public health, etc.) and non-profit agencies, ranging from Boys & Girls Clubs to volunteer and charitable groups.

- **The Media** – Includes both electronic and print media.

The Ten Principles of Community Policing

Reducing community policing to its essence is a challenge. Trojanowicz continued to refine the Ten Principles, and this version reflects work he had completed shortly before his death for a project on implementing community policing in public housing. This is based on an earlier version of the Ten Principles (see Appendix A) and the Nine Ps of community policing (see Appendix B).

- **Change** – Change is the constant that drives the organizational culture and individual behavior to view the transition to community policing as an opportunity to improve the way police services are delivered. Community policing is a significant departure from the status quo, since it requires forging new partnerships with the community and implementing changes within the department that maximize opportunities for everyone to participate in community building and community-based problem solving.

- **Leadership** – Leadership means constantly emphasizing and reinforcing community policing's vision, values, and mission within each organization at all levels. It means everyone within the department must support and promote the commitment to community building and community-based problem solving as the primary police activities. Leadership also implies serving as role models for taking risks and building collaborative relationships to implement community policing, inside and outside the organization. Everyone must exhibit leadership within the opportunities and limits of his or her role and position to influence and educate others about community policing.

- **Vision** – Vision is the picture of the ideal – the image of how we want to improve public safety and quality of life through community policing. This vision, which should include the core values of police personnel and citizens, should provide the inspiration, motivation, and authority to achieve short-term and long-term goals to implement community policing. The vision of community policing is an entirely new philosophy and management approach that influences organizational policies, procedures, and practices.

- **Partnership** – This principle supports the development of equal partnerships among all groups within the community, as a means of promoting collaboration and consensus. Developing community policing partnerships is an organizational philosophy and strategy for community building and problem solving.

- **Problem Solving** – Problem solving is an analytic process and strategy for identifying and pinpointing, in a collaborative manner, specific community situations/events and their causes, so that tailor-made responses may be designed. Problem solving involves an organization-wide commitment to go beyond traditional police responses to crime, to address a multitude of problems that adversely affect quality of life.

- **Equity** – The principle of equity in the delivery of police service recognizes that all citizens will receive effective, respectful police service, regardless of race, gender, ethnicity, religious belief, income, sexual preference, and other differences. Community policing also recognizes the special concerns of specific populations – women, elderly, and juveniles. Moreover, it recognizes that providing equitable service does not always mean providing the same amount or level of service, but that service should reflect need.

- **Trust** – Trust is the conviction that people mean what they say. A community policing organization must demonstrate that it has integrity – that it will follow through on its promises to the community. Trust reduces mutual suspicions of police and residents, and it provides the foundation that allows the police and community to collaborate, and it must be based on mutual understanding and respect.

- **Empowerment** – Empowerment is the act of creating an opportunity for expressions of power and ownership. Community policing creates a shift within the police organization that gives greater autonomy (freedom to make decisions) to line personnel and to the community. Empowering line-level personnel is designed to encourage and support them in collaborative community building and problem solving to assist the community in empowering itself.

- **Service** – This principle expresses community policing's commitment to provide decentralized and personalized police service to neighborhoods, with the intensity and type of service dictated by the needs of the neighborhood. The citizens must be viewed as "customers" by the police. By viewing the citizens as their clients, police can learn, through empathic listening, which services are most needed and when.

- **Accountability** – This principle refers to mutual accountability: the community holds the police accountable for their actions; at the same time, the police hold the community accountable for shouldering its share of the responsibility in promoting and maintaining public safety and the overall quality of life.

What Community Policing Is *Not*

To understand what community policing *is* also requires knowing what it is *not*.

- **Community Policing Is Not a Tactic, Technique, or Program** – Community policing is not a limited effort to be tried and then withdrawn, but instead is a new philosophy of delivering police service to the community.

- **Community Policing Is Not Public Relations** – Improved relations with the community is a welcome by-product of delivering this new form of decentralized and personalized service to the community, rather than its primary goal, as is the case with a public relations effort.

- **Community Policing Is Not Community Harassment** – Merely because a police activity takes place in the community does not make it community policing. Community policing requires working with the community as equal partners in identifying, prioritizing, and solving problems of crime and disorder.

- **Community Policing Is Not Anti-Technology** – Community policing can benefit from new technologies, such as computerized call-management systems, if they provide line officers more free patrol time to engage in community building and community-based problem solving. Computers, cellular phones, telephone answering machines, fax machines, the Internet, and other technological advancements should enhance interaction with the community.

- **Community Policing Is Not "Soft" on Crime** – Community policing addresses the entire matrix of problems that result in crime, fear of crime, and disorder. The distinction is that community policing considers arrest as an important tool in solving problems, not as the primary yardstick of success or failure.

- **Community Policing Is Not Flamboyant** – Dramatic, SWAT-team actions make headlines, but community policing complements such efforts by tackling chronic problems that require long-term community building and community-based problem solving.

- **Community Policing Is Not Paternalistic** – Community policing shifts the role of the police from the "expert" with all the answers to a "partner" in an effort to make the community a better and safer place in which to live and work.

- **Community Policing Is Not Cosmetic** – Community policing deals with real problems: serious crime, illicit drugs, and fear of crime. It does so by addressing the entire range of dynamics that allow such problems to fester and grow.

- **Community Policing Is Not a Top-Down Approach** – Community policing shifts more power, authority, and responsibility to the line level. By shifting power to the bottom of the management pyramid, it means that ideas are more likely to work their way up from the bottom than to be imposed from the top.

- **Community Policing Is Not Just Another Name for Social Work** – Helping to solve people's problems has always been an integral part of policing, at least informally. Community policing merely formalizes and promotes community building and community-based problem solving that includes a strong law enforcement component.

- **Community Policing Is Not Just about Results** – Community policing is about both means and ends. Of course, public safety is the paramount goal, but not if it means repression or coercion. The goal is to ensure that the process promotes fairness, civility, openness, and collaboration, so that everyone has the opportunity to share in both the successes and failures.

- **Community Policing Is Not Elitist** – As Trojanowicz' colleague, the late professor Lou Radelet said, "The goal is to ensure that the police do not stand apart from the community, but that they become a part of the community." Community policing requires the support and/or direct participation of all of the Big Six (see pp. 7-8, this text), with average citizens playing an equal role.

- **Community Policing Is Not Aimed at Any One Social Class** – Critics have argued that community policing shifts a dispropor- tionate amount of police resources to low-income and minority neighborhoods, but proponents argue that equity requires expending resources where they are needed most. It seems clear that some communities have traditionally been underserved by police, and community policing attempts to provide neighbor- hoods the level of policing required to make them safe.

- **Community Policing Is Not "Safe"** – By challenging the status quo and encouraging risk-taking, community policing implicitly includes allowing for failure and embarrassing mistakes.

- **Community Policing Is Not a Quick-Fix Solution or a Panacea** – While creative, community-based problem solving can yield immediate successes, community policing also invests in longer- term community-building strategies designed to solve problems and improve the overall quality of life over time. Especially because of its emphasis on positive intervention with juveniles, the full extent of community policing's impact on the communi- ty may take years to achieve its full potential.

- **Community Policing Is Not Just Another Name for Business as Usual** – If there is no substantive change, then it is not com- munity policing.

- **Community Policing Is Not Synonymous with Problem- Oriented Policing (POP)** – It is possible to do problem-solving policing without the active collaboration of the community, but why would you want to? Admittedly, involving the community as equal partners is more difficult, and it requires more time, but community policing argues that doing so enhances the buy-in of key stakeholders, the quality of the outcomes, and the overall chances of success.

The Theoretical Basis for Community Policing

The question often arises whether community policing is based on accepted theory. Research conducted in the early 1990s by Robert Tro- janowicz' wife Susan (Trojanowicz, S., 1992) proposes that community polic- ing is based on two social science theories: *normative sponsorship theory* and *critical social theory*.

- **Normative Sponsorship Theory** – Normative sponsorship the- ory proposes that most people are of good will and that they will cooperate with others to facilitate the building of consensus

(Sower, 1957). The more that various groups share common values, beliefs, and goals, the more likely it is that they will agree on common goals when they interact together for the purpose of improving their neighborhoods.

- **Critical Social Theory** – Critical social theory focuses on how and why people coalesce to correct and overcome the socioeconomic and political obstacles that prevent them from having their needs met (Fay, 1984). The three core ideas of critical social theory are:

    - **Enlightenment** – People must become educated about their circumstances before they can lobby for change.

    - **Empowerment** – People must take action to improve their condition.

    - **Emancipation** – People can achieve liberation through reflection and social action.

The Ideal versus the Achievable

At any given time, the past and the future live with us. On the one hand are departments that have yet to implement community policing, though their numbers continue to decrease annually. On the other end of that spectrum are departments seeking to take community policing to the next level. For some, this means making community policing so much a fabric of what police do that the efforts are seamlessly woven into everything that the department does, as naturally as breathing. Others view it as moving beyond dealing with immediate crises toward developing more sophisticated initiatives aimed at deep-rooted and hidden problems, such as violence against women and child abuse that perpetuate the cycle of violence.

In between both extremes are the majority of departments working to institutionalize and optimize this promising reform.

- **Department-Wide Philosophy** – Many departments implement community policing in phases. One of the most common scenarios is that the department starts by recruiting volunteers to serve as community policing officers (CPOs) in one or more beat areas, typically located in the "hot spot" areas of the jurisdiction, and then to expand the initiative from there. In the early 1990s, the U.S. Department of Housing and Urban Development (HUD) began providing funding for officers in public housing developments. Then the Crime Act of 1994, through the Community Oriented Police Services (COPS) Office, began making a down payment on its promise of putting 100,000 more officers on the street. In both cases, the funding for additional personnel persuaded many departments to adopt some form of community policing, and both federal efforts offered departments training and technical assistance as well. The good news about the HUD and COPS' investment in community policing was that the new funding provided departments a financial incentive to explore community policing. The bad news, however, was that many departments implemented community policing as a program rather than as a new way for the entire department to deliver service to the community.

Done carefully, with appropriate planning and investment in training, a phased approach can be a realistic way to begin. Even in the best of circumstances, however, the downside to a phased approach that relies on beginning with a handful of CPOs as community policing specialists is that it automatically brings with it all of the issues of split force identified previously. It also makes embracing the community policing philosophy appear optional, as something for which you volunteer.

This is not to say that this phased approach should therefore be abandoned. But it highlights the special challenges inherent in moving from there toward department-wide adoption of the philosophy. As we shall see in the next section on planning, expanding community policing so that it becomes everyone's job must be part of a strategic plan to implement community policing as part of identifying the vision, values, and mission of the department. Conceptualizing what a department-wide commitment will look like in a specific agency takes time and foresight, and many departments are finding that that is a greater challenge than they had anticipated.

- **Citywide Strategy** – As noted above, many police departments gradually introduce community policing by first investing in stationing community policing officers in a few hot-spot beat areas. The danger, of course, is that this risks labeling community policing as valuable only in high-crime, low-income, minority neighborhoods. Of concern as well is that implementing community policing also typically requires reallocating existing resources, for example, by implementing call management. Imagine the resentment when a middle-class family that calls police once a decade, if ever, is now told that an officer will not be immediately dispatched to their home. Why? So that the department can free up resources to station more officers in high-crime neighborhoods. The challenge is to envision a citywide strategy of community policing that enhances police service to all neighborhoods, so that it is not perceived as a program for the poor but a better way of policing for everyone.

- **Institutionalizing Change** – The average tenure of a big-city police chief continues to plummet, now down to between 3½ to 4½ years. At the same time, implementing community policing requires a long-term commitment of at least a decade or more. As this suggests, much of the challenge in implementing community policing stems from the fact that chiefs do not always serve long enough to cement permanent change. Indeed, the short tenure of the chief tends to embolden critics who feel that they can simply outwait a new chief with new ideas.

  The goal therefore is to find ways to institutionalize the changes that community policing demands so that the philosophy will outlive the tenure of the chief. An essential part of this process involves reviewing department policies, practices, and procedures, both to make changes that institutionalize the change to community policing and also to amend or remove those policies, practices, and procedures that contain barriers to full implementation. Consider the case where the chief of a medium-size department believed that the best way to institutionalize community policing was to restructure so that line-level officers would meet regularly as problem-solving teams with members of the community. The problem was that union rules on shift times, overtime, and shift rotation made the system unworkable – the teams could meet only once a month and their roster could change every three months. Without tackling the tough work of changing the rules, the new approach had little chance to "take" before the chief left the following year.

A Zero-Tolerance Approach to Abuse of Authority

In this post-Rodney King/Abner Louima (two well-known cases of excessive force from the West and East coasts, respectively) world of policing, there is a growing awareness that emphasizing the positive (investing in efforts to empower all police to become community builders and problem solvers) must be balanced with a commitment to deal with the negative (dealing with the marginal employee who puts the entire department's gains at risk).

There is reason to believe that forging partnerships with the community at all levels can act as a hedge against brutality, because the community has the opportunity to hold officers individually and collectively accountable. Indeed, citizens often look to civilian review boards as a means of having input into the process, yet such boards rarely have much power. Community policing offers greater opportunities for citizens to have a direct influence in decisionmaking and prevention of problems before they occur.

Yet there will also be the proverbial bad apple who must be dealt with, painful and difficult as that task may be. At an FBI Academy executive training session a few years ago, a Midwest chief confided that this is one of the toughest parts of the job, but one of the most important. He had an officer that he feared was crossing the line. "I could tell something was wrong because other officers no longer wanted to work with him," he said. "And I heard rumblings from the community." Yet the chief delayed, in the hope that the problem would resolve itself. Instead, the officer erupted, murdering his mistress and setting her house on fire in an attempt to cover up the crime. "I promised myself then that, from now on, I want to deal with any concerns about an officer immediately," he said.

The aforementioned Chief Harry Dolan said that one of the best ways for him to monitor how his officers treat citizens is to accompany an officer on the beat at least once a month. "A chief who thinks that he can get a handle on these problems from behind a desk is kidding himself," Dolan says. He remembers the night that he was out with an officer when they stopped a man who had often run afoul of the law. Chief Dolan asked the man how things were going, and he trusted the chief enough to say that one of his officers had hit him a few nights earlier. The man said, "I know the rules – if you don't want a beating, don't run. But I didn't run and he hit me anyhow." Dolan followed up immediately and disciplined the officer.

Dolan remembers when he fired an officer for using his flashlight as a bludgeon without provocation, and some of the officers' friends questioned the decision. "I was the least of his worries. All I did was fire him. In comparison to what I did to him, look at what he did to himself by using that flashlight. He made himself vulnerable to criminal penalties and civil lawsuits that could keep him tied up for years, not to mention how he put the reputation of his fellow officers at risk," said Dolan.

A New Vision

Community policing is a profound change from the past, but it would be a mistake to construe this as a total rejection of the past. Community policing builds on the basic virtues of policing by its strong support for basic policing mandates, such as rapid response to emergency calls, enforcement of prevailing laws, and promoting public safety.

Community policing proposes that it is time to move beyond working harder and faster toward working smarter and working together with the community. In essence, community policing maintains the commitment to putting out the fires whenever and wherever they erupt, but it adds the all-important focus on collaborating with others to alter the conditions that allow fires to occur.

As the continuing declines in the rates of violence attest, community policing offers new answers to longstanding problems. The goal now is to continue building on that success, by strengthening and expanding the coalitions that can be harnessed toward making our communities even safer. Some experts believe that what we are experiencing now may be the lull before a new storm as a large cohort of juveniles begin to reach their most crime-prone years. That adds a sense of urgency in institutionalizing community policing as the way that all police agencies will deliver service to their communities in the twenty-first century.

Questions and Answers

Why do you say that community policing is a philosophy? Community policing is far more than a program, a technique, or a tactic. It instead implies a new way of thinking about how the police operate in the community, focusing as much on means as ends. The particulars of structure and tactics can be different from place to place, but what remains the same is the new way of thinking – the new paradigm – that says that the long-term health of the community depends on the police working as equal partners with the community on the entire spectrum of problems that today's communities face.

Is community policing something new? Community policing is cutting edge in the sense that it offers new solutions to longstanding problems. Yet the elements that make up community policing have existed in some form for a long time. In small towns, officers and citizens often know each other, and they often work together to solve problems. In many ways, community policing formalizes the informal community-based problem solving that has long been the hallmark of small-town policing. As Canada's Chris Braiden says, the police must return to acting as the peacekeepers of the village, and no matter how large the city, it ultimately breaks down into neighborhoods that are the equivalent of villages.

Is community policing unique to the United States? Community policing is a worldwide phenomenon, and it continues to grow and expand. Canada was an early pioneer, and Japan has long had a version of community collaboration suited to its culture. It is interesting to note that community policing chiefs now consult all over the world. Drew Diamond of the Police Executive Research Forum has spent time in Bosnia, assisting in developing a civilian police force. Raymond Kelly, the popular New York City police commissioner who succeeded Lee Brown, did the same in Haiti.

Are there any "model" community policing departments that have demonstrated that this approach is effective and viable over time? Community policing has demonstrated its effectiveness in numerous locations, using many different yardsticks including significant drops in crime rates. Indeed, there are those who say that community policing is at least a significant cause of the overall decline in violent crime since passage of the Crime Bill of 1994. Yet there is no such thing as a "model" that everyone should follow. Community policing should not look the same everywhere, but instead must be tailored to the specific needs and resources of each department and each community.

How long does it take for a police department to make the transition to community policing? Fully institutionalizing community policing may require 10 to 15 years. While that sounds forbidding, as the next section will show, investing time in planning up front can save time and trouble later. Institutionalizing community policing requires re-thinking hiring and selection; training; performance evaluation; and promotion. Moreover, it takes time for people at all levels of the department to become skilled in community-based problem solving and community building. And success also requires a long-term commitment to empower the community so that it can begin to solve its own problems.

Does community policing pose a threat to civil rights? True community policing, where the community is an equal partner, is not only not a threat to civil rights, but a hedge against abuse of authority, invasion of privacy, and excessive force. Community policing depends on building bridges of trust between people and their police. Unfortunately, some police agencies that claim to be doing community policing instead use the term to justify harsh crackdowns on disorder without the support and consent of the people in the target neighborhoods. Not only does that risk a rupture between police and community, but it unfairly tags community policing as embracing tactics that are in conflict with the philosophy.

How does community policing affect officer safety? Research done in Flint, Michigan, decades ago showed that an officer on foot patrol often felt safer than two motor patrol officers together in a patrol car. There were numerous times that community policing officers who found themselves in danger were saved by members of the community who came to their aid. Providing officers the opportunity to develop partnerships with the community is the best insurance they can have.

Can a police department have community policing without community policing officers? Perhaps the better question is: Why would a department want to ignore the opportunity to station specific officers in hot-spot neighborhoods, where they can act as mini-chiefs and mini-mayors, as the department's on-site community builders and problem solvers? If it is because the implementation plan that the department created in partnership with the community relies on other strategies to accomplish those goals, then that is their choice. However, if the department avoids community policing officers because of concerns about internal backlash, perhaps the better choice would be to assist police managers in developing a plan to deal with that problem.

How can police managers deal effectively with the split-force issues that often result from stationing some officers as community policing officers in beats? The ultimate goal is for community policing officers to put themselves out of business, as the communities become empowered and therefore capable of handling their own problems. Until then, however, police managers must make it clear that they will not tolerate any ridicule or sabotage of CPOs and their assignment. They must also require everyone in the department to express the community policing philosophy in their work. At the same time, CPOs must not be perceived as having a "cushy" assignment where they change their hours to suit their personal needs rather than those of the community. CPOs must be full-fledged law enforcement officers who respond to calls in their beats and who make arrests, but the job must provide them the freedom, flexibility, and opportunity to engage in community building and community-based problem solving. The key is that supervisors must ensure that the CPOs focus their energies on problems about which the community cares.

What is the difference between problem-oriented policing and community policing? All community policing involves problem solving, but not all problem-oriented policing is community policing. Problem-oriented policing asks police to work smarter, by analyzing the reason why crimes occur and then to develop strategies to intervene in the dynamics. Combining this proven technique in dealing with problems of crime and disorder with the synergy that comes from collaborating with the community makes community policing an incredibly powerful approach. Admittedly, involving the community in collaborative, community-based problem solving is often a slower and somewhat sloppier process, but the results go beyond what the police alone could ever hope to accomplish.

Notes

1   Murray, Charles, *Images of Fear,* Harper's Magazine (May 1985), p. 41.

2   Wilson, James Q., and Kelling, George L., "Broken Windows," *The Atlantic Monthly* (March 1982) p. 29.

3   Skogan, Wesley E., and Maxfield, Michael G., *Coping with Crime* (Beverly Hills, CA, Sage Publications, 1981) p. 121.

SECTION II
The Planning Process:
A Community Policing
Approach to Change

The Importance of Planning

The adage is that we do not plan to fail – we fail to plan. Nowhere is that truer perhaps than when implementing community policing. In fact, many of the police executives who have attempted to make the transition to community policing agree that, if they have the chance to do it over again, they would invest far more time, energy, and care in planning. A change as profound as community policing, which asks police to re-think their philosophy of policing, requires the greatest possible participation and buy-in, and that requires thoughtfulness and inclusion.

Community policing has now been around long enough to learn from broad experience, and the clearest lesson is that community policing must never be adopted as a limited program, the special job of a handful of volunteer officers whose job is to shoulder the entire burden. If we continue painting this picture of the worst of all possible ways to implement community policing, those officers would be given no training; they would be stationed in huge, high-crime beats; and nothing else would change – they would still be subject to the same top-down management and supervision, and they would still be judged by the same yardsticks (number of calls answered, arrests made, citations issued). Compounding the mistakes even more, there would be no attempt to trumpet whatever successes the officers achieved, but their failures would quickly become fodder for the rumor mill. Worst of all perhaps is that police managers would rapidly distance themselves from the experiment, thereby allowing the critics to undermine and destroy the effort unchallenged.

At least some elements of this prescription for disaster unfortunately ring true in too many cases. It is a testament to community policing's power that some departments have been able to overcome truly shaky starts. Others have, however, become casualties, thereby adding further insult by tarnishing community policing's reputation with their demise. Yet the purpose in outlining this worst-case scenario is that it provides a blueprint, a mirror image of what should happen to maximize opportunities for success.

Leadership at All Levels

Leadership at all levels is crucial in implementing and institutionalizing community policing. Yet confusion persists concerning what leadership means and what it looks like in action. If the community is an equal partner, does this mean that every decision must await their input? Can an individual make a difference in what must clearly be a team effort? Isn't leadership limited to those at the top, the chief and top command, the people with the power?

Defining leadership in the context of community policing means that everyone must share the same vision and everyone can and must find ways to advance that vision through the work. Leadership is not limited to the chief and top command. In fact, many would argue that it is the middle managers and first-line supervisors who have the real power to determine whether community policing succeeds or fails. This chapter will explore all of the elements of planning involved in implementing and institutionalizing community policing, while identifying opportunities for leadership at all levels. Leadership is therefore not something that stands apart from change, but it must be an integral part of each step of the process.

Strategic Planning

It is because community policing is a philosophy and not a program, tactic, or technique that departments must be willing to devote the time, energy, and resources to strategic planning to implement and institutionalize this new form of decentralized and personalized police service. It is a mistake to think that the major planning effort can come later, after an initial experimental phase. As the worst-case scenario shows, a failure to infuse the entire department with the community policing philosophy risks dooming any pilot project. For community policing to thrive, it must be something that everyone understands and does, and not the exclusive province of a handful of officers who risk becoming marginalized.

To begin the continuing dialogue about how best to work with the community, strategic planning offers a blueprint that encourages revisiting the core issues that together define policing. Leadership also means learning by example, and how the planning process is conducted sends a strong message about how community policing works. The strategic planning process itself must therefore reflect the Ten Principles of community policing: change, leadership, vision, partnership, problem solving, equity, trust, empowerment, service, and accountability.

Audit/Needs Assessment

Many police departments recognize the wisdom of conducting audits/needs assessments as an important first step in the planning process. The goal is to establish a baseline against which change can be measured. What are the existing resources in the department and in the community, and where are the strains, gaps, and shortfalls in terms of needs?

Part of the challenge here, as it is with all steps in the planning process, is to make the process itself as inclusive as possible, and to use this opportunity to gather new and different kinds of information. In terms of analyzing where the department stands, the goal is to go beyond simple data collection and analysis of how the budgets for personnel and equipment stack up against the workload. Where are the bottlenecks? How does the department identify and address chronic problems in the community? Which officers feel that their jobs allow them to do a good job and why? What is the profile of the average officer? How has that changed over time? What kinds of skills are valued and rewarded?

Analyzing the community also requires going beyond traditional crime data. What are the demographics of the community? How has that changed over time, and what are projections for the future? What do people think are the biggest problems with crime and disorder in their neighborhoods? What is the business community's perception of safety?

The analysis should go beyond a narrow focus on problems, to include identifying strengths that may have been overlooked. Even the poorest neighborhoods have unique resources. For example, experience in public housing shows that many single mothers are eager to gain documented work skills. If this can be channeled into providing them the chance to volunteer in a substation or local office in exchange for training on office equipment and letters of recommendation, this is a resource beyond what can be found in more affluent suburban communities that everyone abandons during the day to go to work.

Tactics and techniques to conduct audits and needs assessments range from gathering existing data to conducting simple surveys to hosting sophisticated focus groups. Police management continues to benefit from adapting strategies that for-profit companies have used to enhance performance among their own personnel and to better understand their consumers.

Some police departments have been able to form partnerships with local utility companies or newspapers that publish police department surveys free of charge. Others have approached local colleges and universities, offering to serve as case studies for students in marketing who need experience conducting focus groups. Again, the Internet provides a new way for continuous feedback.

A Shared Vision of Positive Change

The challenge in building a map to the future lies in knowing what the destination looks like so that you can see whether you are on the right track. Once you identify where you want to end up, the path to get there becomes clearer. So how do we go about envisioning what a community policing department should look like?

For an innovative training program on Community Policing in Public Housing, offered through the U.S. Department of Housing and Urban Development's Office of Resident Initiatives and the U.S. Department of Justice's Bureau of Justice Administration, participants were actually asked to participate in an envisioning exercise. Participants were told to loosen any tight clothing and even to jettison their shoes. The lights were dimmed. Participants closed their eyes. And then they were asked to envision themselves entering a hot-air balloon in the middle of their towns, a balloon that floated away and then returned five years later. How would the community be different if community policing had been fully implemented in the meantime? How would interactions between people and police look different? What would police be doing in those communities? What would people on the street be doing?

How would "hot spots" have changed? In what ways would the community look different? What about interactions with children? What would be different about specific problems – open drug dealing, prostitution, physical decay of the neighborhood, gangs, idle youth, truancy? How would the community's role in dealing with those problems have changed?

While it may sound hokey, the exercise was always a great success. For one thing, it allows people to disengage themselves from preconceived ideas. It also focuses on the positive. So much of policing focuses on the problems, on the "bad guys," that it is easy to lose sight of the real goal, which is creating a healthy and viable community where both the police and the community accept their fair share of the responsibility.

Important as well is that this exercise was conducted with teams that included not only police but formal and informal community leaders, such as school principals, social workers, hospital administrators, ministers, and community residents. It is worth noting that when the individuals shared their ideas, so that each team produced a shared vision, those teams that included a teacher tended to have a special role for schools. Those that included a hospital administrator, of course, had elements that showed how the hospital had developed a new relationship with the community.

Translating this exercise into a workable format for a specific police agency requires careful thought. The danger is that smaller agencies assume that their close interaction with the community means "we know what they think, so we don't actually need them to join us." Experience instead shows that only through direct and focused interaction does the broadest possible cross-section of ideas and information emerge.

The goal is to develop a plan that provides opportunities and encouragement for everyone at all levels of the Big Six to participate, at least at some level. In smaller departments in smaller communities, the percentage of those who can participate directly will obviously be higher than in major cities, where input must come from representatives who reach out to their constituents. The important thing is to offer as many opportunities for meaningful participation as possible: through meetings inside and outside the department; designating individuals to seek information from their peers; surveys, memos, flyers, and brochures about the process; and encouraging input through telephone calls, letters, E-mail, and through the department's Web site, a wonderful new communications tool.

The emphasis should be as much on "shared" as on "vision." While leadership from the top means that the chief and top command must be clear that this change will happen, the shape of that vision for the future must be a combination of everyone's best efforts. The resulting vision must blend input from the police, the community, elected civic officials, business, public and non-profit agencies, and the media into a seamless whole that provides the focus for the rest of the planning process.

A Backdrop of Mutual Values

It is undeniably possible to make communities safer, with rapid results, through oppressive and repressive police tactics. We have only to look at the example of the Soviet Union to see that a police state can simply impose its will and thereby suppress violent crime. The challenge therefore becomes how to make communities safer in ways that reflect our democratic values and that fulfill the commitment to police the community without violating our legal, moral, and ethical principles.

Revisiting the issue of values as part of the planning process helps to reaffirm how that vision of the future will be achieved, again that the means are as significant as the ends. Community policing does not achieve safety at the expense of civil rights, nor does it jeopardize important values related to honoring communities, families, and individuals. As we will see in a succeeding section, community policing provides police with new opportunities to improve the way they deal with issues of diversity, both internally and externally. Analysis of citizen complaints typically confirms that the issues that matter most to people are often that they are treated with civility, courtesy, sensitivity, and respect. Codifying those values in a *Code of Ethics* helps to institutionalize the ethical framework within which the department will operate.

Defining the Mission

Revisiting the mission of the police as part of the strategic planning process to implement and institutionalize community policing is the first step in operationalizing the vision and values. The goal, of course, is to use this opportunity to create a mission that everyone remembers and understands. Both of the following one-sentence mission statements were created early in the community policing movement, yet they ring as true today as when they were written more than a decade ago:

> **Mission Statement:** "To provide quality police service to our community by promoting a safe environment through police and citizen interaction, with an emphasis on integrity, fairness, and professionalism." *[Produced by the Aurora (CO) Police Department under Chief Jerry Williams.]*

> **Mission Statement:** "To create an atmosphere of safety and security in the Tulsa community, through proper, responsive, community-based police service." *[Produced by the Tulsa (OK) Police Department under Chief Drew Diamond.]*

Many departments elect to print mission statements on the back of peoples' business cards. Some departments also choose to pick key words as a slogan that can be used as the department's motto, emblazoned on everything from patrol cars to awards.

Yet again, it is the process or arriving at the mission statement that is as important as the words selected. If it is done within the context of mutual trust and shared input, it helps to cement the very changes that community policing attempts to implement. But if it is ridiculed by a few as more of that "touchy-feely," social work stuff, then the exercise is futile because it shows that leadership has been unable to create a climate that allows positive change and trust to flourish.

Robert Lunney, who is credited with launching community policing in both Winnipeg and Edmonton in Canada, said that the good news and bad news about police is that they have been trained to take orders. While that can be a curse when police managers want to change behavior and transform police officers into creative, entrepreneurial problem-solvers and risk-takers, it is a blessing when police managers can order the troops to stop complaining and adapt to the need for change.

The Implementation Plan

Returning again to that worst-case scenario, we learned that implementing community policing as a special program not only fails to take full advantage of this powerful form of policing, it risks negatively impacting on community policing far into the future by getting started on the wrong foot. Yet what does it mean to implement community policing as a department-wide philosophy? What does that look like in practice?

Keeping in mind the vision, values, and mission of the department, one way to begin evaluating how community policing should look within any specific department requires identifying the ideal and then working backwards. Consider the captain who said that he would know that community policing was working in his department if the community came to him with a chronic problem and he could relax, confident that a system was in place to guarantee that the problem would be addressed.

Each summer he would receive calls about the escalating potential for youth violence at the city's swimming pools. "I get calls from people in the neighborhood and from the lifeguards at the pool asking for help," he said. "But this year, when I talked to my lieutenants in patrol, they complained that their officers are stretched so thin that they don't know when they could find the time to send someone to visit the lifeguards."

As this suggests, the solution offered by the lieutenant focuses on having an officer or two make a call rather than on developing a collaborative plan to solve the problem. In the section on the community building and community-based problem solving, we will explore how to structure a response that explores all of the dynamics involved. But for the purposes of understanding the issues that must be addressed in the implementation plan, for starters, it is clear that line-level officers need to have the time and opportunity to do more than make one brief visit to poolside.

A community policing approach requires identifying the key stakeholders, and then determining how to involve them in efforts to understand and solve the problem. A brief review of the Big Six shows that the police have a clear stake in the outcome, as do the parents of the youths and the youths who visit the pool. Add to them the City Recreation Department and its lifeguards; people who have homes or businesses located near the pool; and perhaps schools and churches in the area. How can the police become the catalyst to get them involved? How can the department free officers so that they have time to form a partnership with key stakeholders to identify precisely what the problem is and how to address it? What is required for police managers to think in these terms?

What emerges from this cursory exploration of an optimal response are some of the issues that an implementation plan must address. As is often the case, answering one question raises others: Do officers already have sufficient time to engage in community building and community-based problem solving? Has the department done a thorough analysis of free patrol time?

If officers do not have sufficient time, in useful blocks, to engage in these community-based activities, what has to change for that to happen? Among the places to look for answers are:

- **Despecialization** – Is it more important for the department to have officers locked into special assignments – investigation, narcotics, DARE, K-9, crime prevention, school liaison – than to move those officers back into patrol, thereby allowing all officers greater opportunities for community building and problem solving. Are there entire specialties that should be dropped or cut?

- **Call Management** – Many communities have adopted call management as a better way of managing the workload. Calls that previously would have resulted in immediate dispatch of a patrol car may well receive a lower priority. This approach can be controversial, particularly when taxpayers who rarely call police are surprised to find the rules have changed. Yet in this era of "no new taxes," call management offers a fair and equitable way to manage the workflow, if used to allow officers to spend the time needed to address chronic problems.

- **Civilianization and Volunteers** – Most departments have already availed themselves of every opportunity to put civilians into suitable positions, but not all have done their utmost to recruit and train volunteers. One common error is to think only of low-level volunteers, those who answer phones or file papers. Yet there are people with sophisticated computer skills who might assist in crime analysis or in training officers to make the most of their technology. Corporations often have individuals skilled in teaching team building and time management. Local teachers and professors might be willing to hold workshops on report writing.

As the foregoing shows, working backward from a vision of how community policing should operate in practice to deal with specific problems can assist in identifying the issues to consider in answering the question: What is the best organizational structure for our department to optimize community policing's potential?

If the department is to focus on community building and community-based problem solving, how should form follow function? Some departments, for example, have re-visited how to fulfill the investigative function. The North Miami Beach Police Department experimented with eliminating property crime detectives, assigning that function to their community policing officers. In Lansing, Michigan, the department took a different approach, inventing the community policing detective who worked alongside community policing officers on their beats.

Another important part of the response to that question requires re-visiting the issue of management hierarchy. How many layers of management does it take to run an efficient and effective department? As Canadian community policing pioneer Chris Braiden, who now works as a private consultant in Edmonton, argues, one place to start is by looking at the organizational ("org") boxes that identify the structure of the police department, to identify those that could and should be collapsed or erased.

In a bold experiment, the city of Santa Rosa, California, is experimenting with flattening the hierarchy citywide, so that no agency, including police, has more than three layers of management. As Sergeant Gary Negri explains, in one year, the department went from having one chief, three captains, six lieutenants, and 17 sergeants to a structure that includes one chief, six commanders (area and watch) and 20 sergeants. This is still a work in progress, and they are learning a lot as they go. The only way to make this new system work is to expand the responsibility and authority of each position, so that it makes up for the layers lost. Under the new system, for example, sergeants move closer to the executive ranks than to middle management.

This is not to say that these new structures do not cause new stresses and strains, and some may fail. Yet it is only through a willingness to re-think and revisit how to structure a department to implement and institutionalize the community policing philosophy so that it fulfills the department's vision, values, and mission that departments can find solutions.

Policies, Practices, and Procedures

The implementation plan must include a careful review of all existing policies, practices, and procedures, first with an eye toward identifying problems: Do any policies, practices, and procedures impede the implementation of community policing? For example, union rules in one department prevented officers from exercising flexibility in re-scheduling shift hours. The goal was to have officers meet with city officials (during the day), community groups (often at night), and to participate in implementing problem-solving initiatives aimed at drug dealing and prostitution (often late-night). Fortunately, the department faced the challenge as it would any other problem-solving initiative, and they kept at it until they found an answer.

Policies, practices, and procedures also deserve review as well to see whether "tweaking" can enhance their potential even more. If the goal is to empower line-level personnel, for example, changing the rules to allow the officers more freedom to make their own decisions made sense. How can you prune away bureaucratic red tape?

Of particular concern are policies, practices, and procedures that relate to:

- **Recruitment** – What are the skills that a community policing department wants and needs in its officers? Where can such officers be found (criminal justice, social work, education)? What is the strategy to attract the best officers?

- **Selection and Hiring** - Do selection and hiring techniques fulfill the goal of attracting the best officers? If not, how should they be changed?

- **Training** - Does the academy prepare officers properly for this new philosophy of policing? Does field training get rookies off to the best start? What kinds of in-service training do we need to better fulfill community policing's potential? Are there other outside sources of training that the department should explore?

- **Performance Evaluation** - Do performance evaluations reward officers who do their best in community building and problem solving? Have measurements shifted from a focus on quantifying activity to measuring outcomes and results?

- **Promotion** - Do promotional criteria reflect support for community policing? Do those who do their best to fulfill the Ten Principles of community policing rise in the organization over time? (Conversely, do those who reject or attempt to undermine community policing face sanctions?)

- **Honors and Awards** - Does the department formally and informally acknowledge those who go the extra distance to fulfill community policing's potential?

Internal Resistance

The wry joke about community policing is that all too often the last place it is practiced is within the department. A focus on community building and internal problem solving within the agency is a great place to try out those new skills, beginning with the planning process. The key is to develop particular strategies that address internal resistance – not "if" backlash develops, but "when" it erupts.

Different people have different reasons for resisting this far-reaching reform. For some, it is simply human nature to resist any change. Others feel betrayed that the job that they were hired to do has changed, and many see that as an implicit rejection of their life's work in which they have invested their identity and pride. Some quite frankly would like to sabotage the reform because the changes usually mean more work. There is also a strong undercurrent that community policing emasculates the macho image of police, transforming them into social workers. Still others reject the approach on philosophical grounds, arguing that anything that detracts from a focus on finding and arresting the bad guys is basically a waste of time.

As this suggests, there must be different strategies to address different pockets of resistance. The normal reluctance to change can be overcome with strategies that focus on the benefits of community policing. Some will be persuaded if they see positive results in the community, which means that touting community policing's successes inside the agency can be crucial. Others may come on board once they grasp that community policing enhances officer safety. (Early research in Flint, Michigan, confirmed that one officer on foot patrol in a beat where he or she was known felt safer than two officers in a patrol car.) Still others may become community policing advocates if they see that it promotes job enhancement (improving the quality of the work) and job expansion (broadening the scope of the work), which result in increased job satisfaction.

The most challenging individuals to deal with are those who reject community policing for a combination of emotional, intellectual, and philosophical reasons. It would be sheer folly to expect to convert all of them. However, there have been well-known cases where the most hard-bitten, cynical, and highly resistant officers ultimately became "born-again" community policing proselytizers.

Yet the issue is not conversion, but compliance. Critics must not be allowed to undermine or sabotage the changes. Nor should they be allowed to ridicule those who buy into the reform.

Training is an obvious key to bringing resistors on board, but it is not the only answer. Put bluntly, some police managers find it easier to substitute training for direct confrontation. Chief Harry Dolan of Lumberton, North Carolina, widely recognized for dealing with backlash with a balance of humor and skill, stresses that police managers must consistently send the message that this is a community policing department and that those who do not buy into that would benefit from finding another line of work. "We have to be willing to go the extra distance to bring people on board," says Dolan, "But at a certain point, it's time to join the team or leave, because it isn't good for them or for us."

The Devil in the Details

In all fairness, there are instances in which the resistance stems from the fact that police managers fail to appreciate the hurdles and obstacles that complicate implementing change. On the one hand, the chief and top command cannot become bogged down in minutiae. On the other hand, managers must be willing to listen, acknowledge, and help alleviate roadblocks that can make it difficult or impossible for the plan to succeed.

One department built an important part of its new community policing plan on augmenting collaborative problem solving by providing each officer with a laptop computer. The idea was that E-mail would allow members of problem-solving teams to communicate. Yet months later, the laptops had not materialized, and officers were spending far too much time waiting in line for the chance to log on to one of the handful of antiquated stand-alone computers available to check their E-mail. As one officer said, "This is a case where no one in charge thought this thing through. Even when we get the laptops, there is no plan to train the older officers on how to use them. Yet they hold us accountable and say that we are the reason that the new plan isn't working." Community policing promotes "active listening," which asks police to expand beyond their action-oriented, take-charge mode and listen to others, including their co-workers.

According to Trojanowicz, part of the key in implementing community policing is maintaining an appropriate pace of change. "It's like keeping the tension on the line when you hook a fish," Trojanowicz said. "You have to maintain enough tension to reel them in, but not too much too quickly or you risk breaking the line."

Action Planning

Strategic planning to implement and institutionalize community policing is an ongoing process of grappling with complex and important issues. However, as the outline of the changes required begins to take shape, the challenge is to move good ideas into practice through action planning. Action planning takes good ideas and good intentions and puts them into a sequential series of "baby" steps assigned to specific individuals and groups with specific deadlines (see Appendix C).

For example, if part of the implementation plan includes changing to call management, the challenge becomes breaking down that big job into a series of smaller, more manageable steps, with specific assignments and deadlines. The following steps might be taken:

Step 1: Identify stakeholders whose input is essential.

Step 2: Set a date for the initial meeting with stakeholders.

- Identify someone responsible for finding a place for the meeting
  - Establish a deadline
- Identify someone to invite the stakeholders to the meeting
  - Establish a deadline

Step 3: Set up a pre-planning meeting to determine the agenda.

- Review the steps above to begin identifying the individuals, tasks, and deadlines required to set up the pre-planning meeting.

As this attests, action planning often requires stepping back to add even more steps, to ensure thoughtful planning and maximum inclusion. A planning meeting often requires a pre-planning meeting. The meeting itself often requires subsequent de-briefing sessions with others inside and outside the department. The forms included at the end of this section can help you cement the habit of documenting the steps required to reach specific goals in the implementation plan.

Leadership Revisited

Now that the enormity of the task of implementing community policing is clear, it is evident that leadership at all levels is required. The long-range goal is to move beyond implementation toward institutionalizing community policing, so that it survives changes in leadership and all of the other vagaries that can threaten momentum. But what does it mean to exhibit leadership in support of community policing as a captain, a lieutenant, a sergeant, a line officer, a civilian, a community volunteer?

It is a mistake to think that only the chief and top command have power and therefore that only they can lead. (In fact, chiefs soon realize how limited their power truly is.) Certainly, top command has a special obligation to provide leadership, but everyone within the department has a valuable role to play. Think of the lieutenant who shows personal initiative by surveying other departments to see how they handled shift assignments when implementing community policing. Consider the sergeant who loosens the reins and allows his or her officers the freedom to fail. Or the dispatcher who takes the extra time to explain to the "consumer" of police service why sending an officer tomorrow on that cold burglary call makes it possible for the department to devote time to dealing with hidden problems like child abuse and domestic violence. Maybe it is the citizen who volunteers to the reporter how much safer his or her neighborhood is now that officers take the time to come to community meetings and hear about their problems. All show leadership within the scope of their personal power and influence.

Questions and Answers

How much time should planning require? The flippant answer is: more than we give it and more than we could ever find. Yet there is more than a kernel of truth in that statement, since experience shows that investing time up front in planning can prevent grief later. Obviously, there are differences in the timetable for planning depending on the size of the jurisdiction and the department. However, the reality is that, even in the smaller departments, you should devote a minimum of one month to six weeks just for gathering information and developing a planning strategy that answers basic questions: What kinds of information do you need about the department and the community? How will you solicit regular participation and input from within the department and from the community? Who will be directly involved? How will these individuals gather information and input from others? What other kinds of strategies – surveys, focus groups, town hall meetings – make sense? As this shows, the timetable will likely be calculated in months, not weeks. Remember that you can use the time before "launch date" to prepare the department and the community through training and education, so this is not time lost.

What are the biggest mistakes commonly made in planning? Failing to allocate sufficient time and failing to maximize participation and input are the two biggest mistakes commonly made in planning. About the latter, think of the planning process as an opportunity to build support, as a hedge against backlash and dissension. The more that people have an opportunity to participate and see that their ideas are heard, the more they will have a stake in making sure that the plan succeeds. Another major mistake is not to document your action planning steps on paper. For one thing, it helps avoid misunderstandings. Second, it forces you to identify someone who is responsible for the task and determine a due date. We all know how easy it is to walk out otherwise thinking it is the other person's responsibility. And third, documentation is a hedge against problems that can occur when someone gets sick, quits, or goes on vacation. With a written record, other people can be brought up to speed to take his or her place.

How do you identify key stakeholders in the department and in the community? There are individuals who are leaders because of positional power and others because of personal power. Ignoring either is counterproductive. Within the police department and the community, building the list of stakeholders with position power is merely a matter of sitting down and making lists and checking them for completeness. For example, make sure that the stakeholders identified in the department include non-sworn and civilian positions. Identifying and including stakeholders who have personal power is also essential. Think of the sergeant to whom everyone else turns to see whether he or she nods in assent. Ferret out these informal leaders in the community as well. Community empowerment specialist Robin Mitchell of Texas talks about how, in her neighborhood, if you do not get "Miz Fanny" on board, you will have problems, particularly if not including her means that you risk making her an enemy. Finding the powerful sergeants and "Miz Fanny's" can often be done informally, just by asking. Or you can circulate forms asking people to nominate three to five individuals whose ideas and opinions hold influence, then compare lists to determine who the informal leaders are.

Are there special qualities of leadership that some people have and others do not have? Volumes have been written on leadership qualities, but the challenge is to enhance individual leadership. We all have the power to influence those around us. Some do it through humor, while others do it through quiet example. If it is to fulfill its potential, everyone has to find ways to express commitment to the philosophy and practice of community policing.

SECTION III
A Formula for Success
Community Policing = LEADERSHIP (Community Building + Problem Solving)

An Overview of the Work

Armed with an understanding of the philosophy of community policing and its Ten Principles, and with the specific vision, values, and mission of the department, the question then becomes – so how does this work? How do those concepts relate to what the police actually do differently in a community policing department? How do you operationalize and optimize the community policing philosophy in practice?

Reduced to its essence, community policing asks police to concentrate their activities on leadership, building community, and solving problems. Leadership is the style/form, and community building and problem solving are the substance/functions. All activity within the department must fall under one of these three categories or support them. Anything else that does not support these goals is a waste of time.

While that sounds simple, remember that community policing profoundly expands the mandate of the police – or at least, it acknowledges that the police have always done more than focus on that narrow band of incidents called crime, since the vast majority of calls for service do not involve crime. Community policing asks the department to collaborate with the community to find solutions to the broad range of problems that they face.

Prior to community policing, the focus of police activity was on answering calls – rapid response – and investigating incidents, both of which fall under community-based problem solving. Yet all too often, the emphasis was more on making the call and filing reports than on solving the problem. The goal for the officer was to get back into service quickly, to be ready to take the next call, rather than on whether the response resolved the situation and satisfied the "customer."

This is in no way intended to denigrate or disparage the officers, the vast majority of whom always wanted to do their best, but the incentives rewarded activity over effectiveness. The officers were responding to supervisors who were pressured to work through the call load on each shift, and those supervisors were merely responding to imperatives from top command to manage the workload by processing calls and taking reports.

The Essence of Leadership

Leadership means announcing that it is time to stand back and plan for change rather than to keep doing more of the same, only faster. Leadership means educating everyone inside and outside the agency about why it makes sense to substitute working smarter and working in partnership for simply working harder. Leadership also means organizing the resources of the department in support of the changes, and providing constant reinforcement so that the changes become operationalized and institutionalized.

It is commonly accepted that it is the community and not the police that has the most power to make communities safer, and the community also has the most to lose or gain since they will bear the consequences. The police cannot simply respond more quickly to keep up with an escalating 911 call load and expect to produce quality. They must at least invest the time to involve the community in dealing with chronic problems, with the goal of reducing the call load over time.

Chief Don Carter of Champaign, Illinois, uses the image of a house to explain the dilemma. The roof is beginning to leak and there is a window in back that needs repair, but how does one justify taking the time to deal with those problems when the front porch is on fire?

This argument made more sense when the rates of violence kept climbing. However, there is an inevitable period of strain that occurs during the time that community policing is being implemented and before community building and problem solving pay off in reducing the rates of crime and disorder. (In fact, the initial outreach into the community often uncovers crime problems that would otherwise have gone unreported.

Implementation of community policing asks the department to reorganize so that after putting out the fire on the front porch, the officers have the time, skills, and commitment to collaborate with the homeowner to repair the broken window and eventually the leaky roof, employing problem-solving techniques that may well require others to help. Spending more time with that homeowner may produce an even longer list of things that need to be repaired, but building that sense of community and solving problems should be the challenge and the satisfaction of the job.

The Issue of Free Patrol Time

Many critics still insist that their department does not have the time to do community building and problem solving. But without an analysis of free patrol time, how can a department know where it stands? How busy is busy?

When former Tulsa Chief Drew Diamond of the Police Executive Research Forum works with departments to implement community policing, he challenges them to think of community policing as an opportunity to treat every situation with the same diligence and care that a homicide typically receives. Usually, he finds himself met with the lament, "But we don't have the time."

"So I have the officers go through the exercise of listing out what they do in a typical day. Pretty soon it becomes clear that the time is there," he says. "As an insider, I can make the case that we can find the time if we want to. Too many officers have begun to think that the time between calls is theirs. The issue is developing the leadership and the will to use the time to go the extra distance."

Another by-product of the good news about recent reductions in rates of violent crime is that they not only prove community policing's value, but they should provide enough of a respite that no one can fall back on the excuse that there is not enough time to do the job well. The expectation is that, over time, community policing will continue to make communities better and safer places in which to live and work, freeing up even more police time for imaginative community building and problem solving.

Making It Happen

Operationalizing leadership at all levels means that any person should use all of the skills and commitment that he or she possesses to make change happen, survive, and thrive. A chief like Harry Dolan inspires through humor and warmth. Former federal drug czar Lee Brown initiated change in Atlanta, Houston, and New York by the force of his logic and dedication, as well as his commitment to producing detailed, written plans as blueprints for the future. A chief like Drew Diamond exhibits a quiet but intense passion that wins converts who want police to be more effective in protecting and empowering everyone in the community, from the richest to the poorest.

The leadership style depends on the personality, attributes, and skills of the individual, but the commitment to change characterizes the thousands of officers at all levels and the citizens in communities who advance the marker an inch or more every day by exhibiting the leadership in their positions:

- **The Chief** – The chief serves as the most visible symbol of the continuing commitment to change. The biggest challenge is to provide sustained leadership both inside and outside the department. That means reinforcing the message constantly, often by jumping the chain of command to make sure that the commitment at the top of the organization is believed and expressed at the bottom. As the face of the department in the community, the chief must also be committed to explaining to the community why this change is necessary and how it will ultimately benefit them, particularly those who feel that they are losers under this new philosophy.

- **Top Command** – Leadership at this level reflects many of the responsibilities of the chief, as well as the challenge of operationalizing planning as a continuous process that ensures that the changes are always being reviewed and modified to enhance success. The chief paints in broad strokes, and top command translates them into action steps. The difficult line that top command must walk requires distinguishing between the need to amend plans and revise policies, practices, and procedures to enhance performance and the danger of "getting rolled," which means allowing critics to sabotage the commitment to change. In essence, it is the job of top command to advise the chief whether the inevitable complaints are valid concerns that should be addressed and those that amount to whining and grumbling (some of which is inevitable with any change). The balance requires standing firm in the basic commitment for community policing, while tweaking the system to make it work as intended.

- **Middle Managers and First-Line Supervisors** – This is the layer of the sandwich that can feel squeezed between the pressure for change from above and the resistance from peers and subordinates, particularly as the inevitable "devils in the details" erupt. No matter how good the plan, there will always be policies, practices, or procedures that need further refinement to make the overall changes work. If the department has done a good job of employing community policing internally, this group will be committed to the change, and mutual trust will allow middle managers and first-line supervisors to collaborate with those above and below them to find ways to overcome the barriers. The danger is that this group's valid concerns will be dismissed as whining or grumbling – or that their whining and grumbling are treated as valid concerns. Moreover if this group encourages, cajoles, and does whatever it takes to sell the concept to the troops, it cannot help but succeed. If they allow whining and grumbling from below, however, this is a prescription for serious problems.

- **Line-Level Officers** - This is literally where the rubber meets the road, the group that must become energized about new opportunities to exhibit leadership within the department and in the community. Empowerment is often dismissed as a buzzword, but that is only because it has been misused to hype business-as-usual masquerading as change. Empowering line-level officers means that they can initiate an effort to engage in community building and problem solving with the community and that their ideas will be heard. Leadership means that even when a peer says, "Why would you want to make more work for yourself?," the officer responds with a quip or a heartfelt statement or whatever it takes to sell the idea that investing the effort in quality policing is its own reward.

The Elements of Community Building

While the focus of today's resistance tends to surround arguments about time and resources, the activities that still rankle community policing's critics the most tend to be examples of community building – shepherding youngsters on a trip, organizing summer sports leagues, visiting senior citizens centers, meeting with crime victims' groups. As one officer said, "Here I am rolling around on the ground at night with drunks, while these guys are out taking kids on the rollercoaster."

What possible rationale can there be for having police officers, at their rate of pay, making what appear to be courtesy calls and babysitting kids? Why shouldn't police activity be focused exclusively on problem solving instead?

At first blush, the arguments sound plausible. However, we must remember that there is general agreement that the community has far more power than the police to control and reduce crime. If we return to that metaphor of the house, it is the homeowner who lives there who has the most time, incentive, and opportunity for home improvements. The goal should be to develop a relationship of trust and partnership, so that over time, working together provides the homeowner the resources and skills needed to do more and more of the job himself. Community policing is even more ambitious by employing community building to enlist teams of people willing to help and learn.

What has often been lost in the discussion about community policing is the goal of community building. It isn't merely a public-relations effort, designed to win friends in the community by doing fun things. It is a serious strategy designed to use police officers as the catalyst in community building, particularly in neighborhoods where there is little or no existing structure. Indeed, the lack of community cohesion is at least part of why the area suffers a disproportionate share of problems. It also offers a strategy to lure back those groups that have become estranged from police.

The first question about community building is often: Why police? Why not other groups in the community? The two best answers are: (1) that it is in the enlightened self-interest of police to help make the community safer and (2) no one else has yet stepped up to the plate to do the job. As Officer Don Christy of the Lansing Police Department often said, "The community wanted someone with some authority and some contacts who could help, and I looked around and there was only me."

Christy became famous for going the extra mile in community building. He established an alcohol-free New Year's Eve party for families, with donated food and music, where police officers greeted guests in tuxedoes. He enlisted a broad cross section of businesses, public agencies, and non-profit groups to help with his annual summer campout. Held in the playground of an inner-city school, this initiative, for one night, transformed the area into a wilderness experience. Kids would sit on bales of hay to roast weenies over the fire. Police officers and politicians pitched in to entertain the kids with everything from a puppet show to magic to a sing-along. Families were able to spend the night together in tents erected by the National Guard.

Christy, however, became a lightning rod for dissent and a target of backlash. It even reached the point where mentioning his name on the police radio risked unleashing a flurry of spiteful jokes about how he was probably off somewhere planting flowers. It seemed that the more Christy exercised his creativity and autonomy, the more he sparked resentment as the poster boy for how community policing wasted time better spent building a case to raid a crack house.

The problem that police managers faced was in explaining why such activities made sense as part of a long-term strategy to address serious crime. Without using the concept of community building as an integral part of a two-pronged strategy with problem solving, those events made a convenient target for critics.

Some will always dismiss the term community building as mere rhetoric to justify activities that police should not do. Yet if we look at the results, the value of community building becomes clear. Officer Christy took neighborhoods that had no identity, no sense of community, and virtually no self-esteem, and he helped them discover all three. One of his initial activities was to host a contest where the neighborhoods chose a name for themselves, such as Sparrow Estates.

Community events brought people together as partners with the police; helped the community recognize its power and abilities; allowed the department to identify and form partnerships with community leaders; and served as a springboard for problem solving with the participation and support of the Big Six. Just in the process of coming together, the community confronted and solved a number of problems, as a by-product of collaboration.

One local resident talked about why she became involved. "I would look out my window during the day and watch this little 12-year-old girl driving in circles on her bicycle," she said. "I could also see her pimp sitting and standing on the curb. I would call the department, but whenever a patrol car turned the corner, they would scatter." Day after day, nothing changed, and her confidence in the ability of the police to solve problems began to wane. It was Officer Christy's community-building efforts that lured her into working with police, which led to solving the problem of the child prostitute.

"People can sometimes have a hard time seeing the connection between holding a picnic and dealing with serious crime," says Christy. "But I have seen how one supports the other."

Outreach to Specific Populations

When we talk about groups that are underserved by the police, the issue is not always geography but diversity - race, class, gender, age, ethnicity, religion, sexual preference. In the past, women have found themselves frustrated that their complaints were not taken seriously, whether the problem was domestic violence, stalking, or sexual assault. Gays rightfully feared being on their own in dealing with gay bashing. "That's your problem." "There's nothing we can do." Community policing challenges the department to do better.

The image of juveniles is often as perpetrators, when the reality is that this age group suffers the highest rates of violence. What answers do police have for kids who are bullied? We see that kids join gangs because they want money, status, friends, identity - and protection. How can the police and the community do more to provide healthy alternatives?

On the other end of the age spectrum are the elderly in high-crime neighborhoods whose physical fragility puts them at special risk. Far too often, they reduce the likelihood of victimization by reducing exposure. Many can only be lured back out into the community once they trust that they will be safe.

Minorities have long argued that all that they want is to be treated with the same respect and dignity that police automatically afford others. Many citizens look to civilian review boards as the key in restraining disrespect, police abuse of authority, and excessive force. Yet that practical reality is that civilian review boards will never be given the power to fulfill the community's full agenda. Community policing can be a far more potent way for the community to hold officers directly accountable and break down barriers on both sides.

Community building is an essential first step in building bridges of trust to groups that have been underserved. Community building is the only way to make the outreach that can build the trust required to involve them in initiatives where their participation is crucial.

Community-Based Problem Solving

If leadership is the "head" of community policing, then community building and community-based problem solving are the two legs that must work in tandem so that the department can take its first baby steps, learn to walk, and then hit full stride.

The problem-solving function of the police covers everything from rapid response to crime analysis to focused problem-oriented initiatives, and community policing expands the definition of the problem to include crime, drugs, social and physical disorder, and fear of crime – the broad array of social ills that afflict contemporary communities.

Community policing therefore brings leadership to community-based efforts to bring police and formal and informal community leaders together in structured problem-solving sessions to deal with specific problems. The Police Executive Research Forum (PERF) in particular deserves recognition for promoting and perfecting Problem-Oriented Policing (POP) as conceptualized by Professor Herman Goldstein of the University of Wisconsin School of Law, to which community policing adds value by emphasizing the importance of bringing community stakeholders directly into the process.

As noted previously, of concern is the tendency for departments to treat community policing as a salad bar from which they can choose only those items they like. Of course, it is possible for the police, by themselves back at headquarters, to engage in problem solving, but why ignore and exclude the power of the community? And, yes, of course, involving the community typically adds to both the timetable and the frustration level. But if we understand that the police can never have all the answers and we want communities to become empowered, how can anyone justify keeping them from the seats at the table where they belong?

Quality-of-Life Concerns

While there is always debate about cause and effect, most would agree that community policing has contributed, at least in part, to recent downswings in violent crime. Yet debate continues to surround which definitions or elements of community policing deserve the credit.

There is little doubt that addressing so-called *quality-of-life* concerns has had an impact. In New York City, for example, fingerprints taken from a man who jumped a subway turnstile led to his arrest later after a murderous assault on a woman that would probably have been solved no other way. Prior to community policing, arresting and fingerprinting subway cheats would have been considered a waste of time.

Yet community policing is also about means and ends. Cracking down on quality-of-life infractions in the community works best when it is done in concert with the community, not just with their tacit consent, but with their direct participation. The goal is not to single out New York City for criticism, but the fact is that critics point to the rise in citizen complaints and the concerns of specific groups, such as artists, that they are targeted for harassment when they are not the problem. The virtue of involving the community directly before and during problem-solving initiatives aimed at quality-of-life concerns is that doing so also promotes that sense of mutual accountability that reinforces restraint.

Crime-Specific Policing

There was a flurry of talk in some places, notably Houston, Texas, that *crime-specific policing* could be an effective alternative to community policing. The idea was that you could strip away the work with the community and focus on working smarter on a specific crime category. This again casts police in the role of the experts, who confer amongst themselves to develop strategies that they then launch in the community. As noted previously, if the goal is to suppress crime rates quickly, even outright heavy-handedness will work, at least for a while. Sadly, however, part of the reason for the decrease may well be that citizens in neighborhoods likely to have these experiments unleashed upon them may simply opt not to call police anymore for minor concerns.

The fact remains that working smarter is only one-half of the answer, and that working together with the community offers benefits beyond ups and downs in the crime rate. It provides a foundation for the trust required for people to share much-needed information with police, and it acts as a hedge against abuse and misbehavior on both sides.

Approaching Problems in the Community

Once community building has helped to bridge the gap between the police and the community, it is time to capitalize on those new partnerships by engaging in focused problem solving. PERF again deserves acclaim for bringing Herman Goldstein's SARA model to police departments, with its sophisticated framework of Scanning-Analysis-Response-Assessment. SARA offers a phased and structured process for addressing problems in the community in a coherent and intelligent way, with opportunities for constant feedback and adjustment at every step.

It is not possible here to do justice to the elegance of the SARA model with all of its nuances. Stripped to its bare essentials, however, it still provides an effective way to approach any problem that police may encounter, from drug dealing on the corner to problems with internal dissent:

- **Scanning** – Stakeholders must gather as much information about the problem as possible: official data, background and demographic information, surveys, personal impressions, news accounts. The goal is to paint a picture in the way that a journalist does – who, what, when, and where (leaving the how and why for later). Imagine how different the kinds of information collected might be if we use street-corner drug dealing as one example and domestic violence as another.

- **Analysis** – Here is where the problem-solving team deals with the how and why. How does a couple's dispute escalate into violence – what are the steps that normally occur? Why does drug dealing occur on this particular corner? The goal is to keep turning the problem around to examine it from different angles to discern the dynamics that allow it to persist.

- **Response** – The group brainstorms ideas and eventually narrows them into a plan, with specific assignments and deadlines. The goal initially is to let everyone's imagination run wild – then to pull back to see what is legal, ethical, and doable. Important as well is to decide in what order the elements of the plan will be attempted. Then it is back to the feedback loops – who else's input would be helpful? Are there dynamics that we are overlooking? Two common mistakes are: (1) to allow the group to jump to the response phase before they have completed a thorough job of scanning and analysis and (2) the impulse on the part of action-oriented police to jump in to save the day by themselves – or to give orders to others rather than to listen.

- **Assessment** – This all-too-often neglected phase asks the group to develop a system for constant monitoring of the plan as it unfolds and to determine a strategy for assessing its impact. How will you determine success or failure? Often, the mistake is to think that success requires eradicating the problem, when the reality is that success can wear many faces. With drug-dealing on the corner, success could mean that buyers from outside the neighborhood are now afraid to stop, for fear of arrest. Maybe the dealers move indoors, which has the benefit of making the street safer and making it harder for casual and first-time users to get hooked. Perhaps the drug clinic shows an increase in people seeking treatment. Or the failure offers clues about what might work in the future. As this suggests, if you do not know where to look to document the different kinds of successes, you risk not finding them.

This list looks deceptively simple and easy to work through, but done properly, it takes time, energy, and commitment. In practice, it moves groups beyond knee-jerk solutions into creating new solutions to chronic problems.

Overcoming Barriers

The aforementioned Drew Diamond created this list of barriers against which a response plan must be judged:

- **People** – Do you have enough people? The right people? The wrong people? Some of the right people and some of the wrong people? Do they have the right skills?

- **Policies, Practices, and Procedures** – Do any pose problems that could sabotage the effort? Are there any that should be modified to improve the likelihood of success?

- **Legal** – As well as moral and ethical constraints.

- **Money** – Are there direct or indirect costs, and is there sufficient money in the budget? Are there other resources in short supply?

- **Politics** – Often the biggest hurdle, and one of the toughest to anticipate and confront.

- **Other** – Any other hurdles that could threaten success? What is it that you have not thought of?

This is not to suggest that barriers are insurmountable. In fact, applying the same problem-solving framework can generate creative ways to overcome these barriers.

It is also not unusual at this stage for a group to discover that one of the barriers is actually the real problem that must be confronted first. A common example is when a group at a North Carolina training session on implementing community policing in public housing initially decided that an open-air drug market in the neighborhood was the problem that needed attention. Once they reached the barrier stage and talked about people, they decided that community involvement was the real problem that they should tackle first. Re-defining the problem or selecting a different problem should always be an option.

How Problem Solving Works in Practice

The good news is that so many police departments have applied community-based problem solving to common problems such as drug-dealing on the corner that it has almost reached the status of a cliché. *Add streetlights, change traffic patterns, and build speed bumps to make incoming customers nervous. Consider seizing at least some of the cars that customers use under forfeiture laws. Beef up police presence and work with the community to set up citizen patrols. Clean up, paint up, fix up. Provide alternative activities for youth. Use fences and barricades to make the site less inviting to foot traffic.* The bad news, however, is that many of these common responses have become so well known that police do not always see the virtue of going through the process with the community themselves, and they try to pick and choose items from this menu.

Fortunately, the crisis of violence related to drug trafficking appears to be waning, many would argue at least in part because of community policing, so we may well see problem-solving techniques applied to a wider range of community problems. One of the most pernicious is domestic violence, since it perpetuates its misery on succeeding generations, adding to the perpetual climate of violence in our homes and on our streets. The following will briefly describe how the community-based problem solving can address this concern.

With support from the U.S. Department of Justice's Office of Community Oriented Police Services (COPS) and the Violence Against Women Grant Office (VAWGO), the Police Executive Research Forum has assembled a team to produce a training curriculum on applying community policing to the problems of violence against women, for which co-author Bonnie Bucqueroux serves as a consultant. The initiative will bring teams comprised of police executives and community advocates who deal with sexual assault, stalking, and domestic violence to the training, where they will be asked to apply problem-solving techniques to specific problems in their jurisdictions.

As an example, let us suppose that one of those teams decides that their goal is to identify and approach the women victimized by domestic violence who do not report their problems to police. The goal in doing so is to see how they could work on new interventions that might help them. So the problem at hand is: Who are these hidden victims of domestic violence and how do we approach them about joining us to solve the problem?

- **Scanning** – Where do you find information about this hidden group? What predictors will give reliable information about women of various educational and income levels and the levels of abuse they suffer? What kinds of abuse do these women suffer? How often? How serious? Who are their abusers? Who knows about the abuse? Are there groups or organizations in the community that might have information about hidden domestic abuse? Do these women have children? Would their schoolteachers know? Do emergency room personnel actually report suspected abuse? Is there more than one profile that could be developed? Who knows their secrets?

- **Analysis** – Why do women decide not to turn to police? Who else do they turn to and why? What different kinds of coping mechanisms do these women use and how effective are they? What makes them approachable and unapproachable? When are they most approachable? How do the abusers conspire to keep them silent? What factors can be changed and which cannot? Are women with children more likely to seek help? How can we make these women feel safe in working with us? (Do we need more information? Should we go back to the scanning phase? Are there other stakeholders whose input is beneficial?)

- **Response** – How do we find these women? Where do we go to make contact? Who should approach them and how? What are we asking them to do? What are we offering? How do we overcome the barriers that we think prevent them from seeking police help? How must police change to earn trust? Who can facilitate positive encounters? How do we ensure that we are not putting these women at greater risk by our actions? How do we get the message out that we want to work with them to find answers? (Do we need to return to the scanning and analysis phases before outlining action steps? Are there others who should be brought into the process?)

- **Assessment** – What will success look like? How will we know if we have reached this target group? What is our expectation of success in terms of how many of these women will agree to work with us? How will we determine whether to revise our response?

This brief list only whets the appetite for more. Keep in mind as well that the answer to any one question is likely to raise a dozen more, and that the group has the right to modify the problem definition or substitute a different problem. The process then focuses on developing an action plan, similar to the one used in planning, with specific assignments, timetables, milestones, and dates.

Moving to Collaboration and Consensus

The next challenge is to adopt the most effective ways to work together. The goal is to move beyond the relatively pallid forms of interchange of *coordination* and *cooperation*, toward true *collaboration*.

- **Coordination** – This promises little more than that people will let each other know what they are doing independent of each other.

- **Cooperation** – This implies a somewhat stronger bond, where people vow to give a helping hand to each other with basic goodwill.

- **Collaboration** – This is the most potent form of interaction, where people commit to working side-by-side as equal partners.

For community-based problem solving to be effective, the participants should never settle for mere coordination and cooperation. But the challenge is how to achieve collaboration, particularly when participants can come from vastly different backgrounds and experience. The danger is often that action-oriented police and other educated professionals may well dominate the decisionmaking as compared to community residents who have less experience in such settings and who may feel insecure.

Reaching Consensus

Another essential element that offers a process for dealing with this dynamic is *consensus,* which means that everyone must agree with the plan. The goal of achieving consensus deserves greater discussion. Many people think of consensus as something that you strive for but abandon if a deadlock occurs. Others insist that consensus means what it says – that everyone must buy into or at least tolerate the plan or it should not go forward.

The argument opposing consensus is that, in a democracy, the side with just one more vote carries the day. That model is held up as the ideal of fairness. The argument in favor of consensus, however, is that, at the grass-roots level, unless you have agreement among all of the groups affected, the plan may not work as well as it could – and it may therefore not work at all.

The following is offered as one way of operationalizing consensus. An alternative school in Bedford, Massachusetts, uses a voting strategy that asks stakeholders to hold up one, two, or three fingers. Three fingers signify strong support; two fingers signify consent; one finger essentially signifies a veto – unless the person can be brought on board, the plan does not go forward.

Using fingers instead of words to vote is an integral part of their process, since it is perceived as less likely to spark acrimony. As one of the teachers who favors this approach says, "It can slow down the process, because it allows one person to hold everyone else up. But it is the fairest system we've found." When a "veto" occurs, sometimes the best bet is to end the meeting to see whether compromises can be worked out before the groups gets together again. "When we go forward, we really know that every stakeholder will give us support."

Making the Pieces Fit

The challenge in this section has been to paint the picture of a formula for success with strokes detailed enough to allow a clear image to emerge, recognizing that each department's portrait of change will look different.

Carrying the analogy even further, community policing asks departments to go beyond a paint-by-numbers, one-size-fits-all approach. Many agencies opt to station community policing officers in beats, at least in the hottest of the hot spots. Others explore instituting community-based problem-solving teams. A number of departments are instituting substations or mini-stations as part of their implementation goal of decentralization. Still others are collaborating with other service providers to open Neighborhood Network Centers where community policing becomes part of Community-Oriented Public Service (a different kind of COPS).

Done properly, through leadership committed to community building and problem solving, these efforts will ultimately succeed, even if that means repeatedly returning to the drawing board to make them work.

Questions and Answers

What does leadership in service of community policing look like in action in a department? The style can differ, depending on the personality of the individual and the culture of the department as a whole. But the substance of leadership is that it provides sustained support and reinforcement at all levels for the changes that community policing demands. Leadership is when the chief walks the beat with an officer one night a month to see what change looks like at the street level (and to set an example by doing so). It can be the sergeant who interjects, "Hey, enough with the grumbling – let's find a way to (get this pregnant woman into drug rehab)(solve the string of break-ins)(*you fill in the blanks*)." It is the officer who makes one more call and finds an area business willing to donate the door prizes for the community picnic. Or the representative of the police bargaining unit who initiates a brainstorming session with his or her peers on how they can be part of making the new approach work. And leadership is the person in the community who has been wary of police who takes a chance and offers to help.

What about the common complaint that there is not enough time for community building and problem solving? A major goal of the implementation plan should be to enhance the time for these activities, which often means reducing the number of specialty assignments and flattening the hierarchy to put more officers into the community. It can mean instituting or revisiting call management, so that priority calls receive the immediate response they deserve, while others become more negotiable. The process also includes reviewing policies, practices, and procedures to make sure that they support community building and problem solving. Yet most important of all is commitment to leadership at all levels to make these activities happen within the resources available. The workload in a laid-back rural area or an affluent suburb with relatively little serious crime is admittedly a far cry from that in an understaffed inner-city precinct or mini-station. But the challenge remains making the transition to working with others and working smarter within the resources available.

How do we decide whether we should invest in a substation, a neighborhood storefront, or some other strategy to move closer to the community? This is a perfect example of the kinds of choices that must be made as part of the planning process, to tailor the response to the specifics within the jurisdiction. The question is: How do we move closer to the community? The answer must reflect the wants and needs of the specific department and community. Particularly in a time crunch, there can be a tremendous temptation to borrow and modify an implementation plan from another department. But the planning process itself serves as a model for how leadership, community building, and problem solving work, and the particulars of any plan must reflect the best thinking of the department and the community.

How much time should be devoted to community building versus problem solving? There can be no hard-and-fast rule, because needs vary so much. Community building is designed to overcome citizen apathy and build trust, help identify formal and informal leadership, and assist in building community leadership where none exists. However, police managers have a responsibility to ensure that community building is put to good purpose in providing the foundation community-based problem-solving initiatives. Organizing recreational and educational activities for young people can be more enjoyable than tackling the tough problem of child abuse, but one must provide the foundation for the other.

When does a problem rise to the level of requiring a full-blown problem-solving approach? If the problem is that a bumper is lying in the middle of the intersection, you move the bumper immediately, without asking for input and collaboration. However, if the problem is that there is a rash of accidents at the intersection for which the solution is not that simple, it is time to talk with residents, shopkeepers, and traffic engineers about collaborating on some solutions. A common failure with action-oriented police, however, is that they can be too quick to want to implement their own solutions, either by short-circuiting the entire problem-solving process, imposing their ideas at the response stage, or by failing to take full advantage of others willing to help. Police managers must be conscientious to remind them that the goal is to share the load with others.

SECTION IV
Building Partnerships
with the Community

Defining Community

Any attempt to explain and define community policing must address what the word "community" means in this context. There is no simple, one-sentence definition, because community can mean very different things to different people.

Understanding the dynamics of "community" is critical to the prevention and control of crime and disorder, as well as fear of crime. How people behave depends on a continuum of influences and determinants that ranges from personal responsibility to informal and formal social control. Individual responsibility is still the most potent factor in determining personal behavior. Conscience keeps people from crossing the line into committing crimes even when no one is looking.

The family is the next most important unit in social control. In addition to its immediate influence on behavior, the family assists youngsters in the initial formation of the conscience and a continued reinforcement of values that encourage (or discourage) law-abiding behavior. Influential as well are the extended family (especially members who live close by) and neighbors. Both can be important in supporting the norms of positive behavior.

Along with social institutions such as churches and schools, this geographic community of families, and neighbors, who typically share the same values, has long been a potent force in modeling and controlling individual personal behavior. Even those who are not pulled back by individual conscience often find themselves restrained by the thought that their behavior would violate the norms of the community and that the community would hold the individual accountable. A cohesive community has a range of informal sanctions that can be imposed for transgressions that range from shame to shunning. In strong communities, individuals understand that there are serious consequences for deviance.

Unfortunately, as families fracture and scatter and as neighbors become nameless strangers, the informal social control of the geographic community has weakened. The advent of mass transportation and modern communication makes us more likely to be part of a *community of interest* rather than one of geography. When we feel lonely or upset, we are as likely to call a neighbor across the country – or pour out our troubles in a global chat room on the Internet – as we are to visit the neighbor next door. This has obvious implications for the ability of the community to control our behavior and to model behavior for the next generation. It is not that our ties to a community of interest do not run deep, but they do not have the geographic focus that allows them to restrain or modify behavior by constant close supervision. As a result, we now find ourselves relying more and more on external, formal social control – in the form of the criminal justice system – for answers to problems that were once the province of the community.

Loosening the bonds of the geographic community no doubt played at least some role in the surge of violent crime that occurred in the late 1960s, when not only did the rates of crime rise dramatically, so did stranger-on-stranger crime. Random crime further contributes to fear and danger that makes people feel that they no longer control their destiny.

Social scientists continue to debate the reasons for this upswing in violence. Children were increasingly being raised in nuclear families and not the extended families of old. Rising divorce rates and the increase in births out of wedlock produced a steady rise in the number of children being raised in single-family homes, often with mothers whose gender put them at an economic disadvantage. While not all families nurture and support their young, the fact remains that raising children is such a demanding task that the more people in the home, the greater the resources and the more that the workload and responsibility can be shared.

At the same time, television and popular culture began to bombard young people with images of violence unlike anything seen before. Although it is the nature of a teenager to assert growing independence and begin the process of moving away from family control and toward individualism, as these youngsters enter their most crime-prone years, the decline in influence of the community undeniably contributed to a dramatic rise in crime in the late 1960s.

We have good reason to be thankful that crime rates are dropping again in the latter half of the 1990s, as compared to the horrific levels of violence that began the mid-1980s with the invention of crack. But the sad fact is that those declines merely return us to the frightening levels of violence that the culture began to suffer in the late 1960s, and not to the substantially safer levels of the 1940s and 1950s.

Many who grew up in that era nostalgically long for a return to those safer "Ozzie-and-Harriet" days. While the pendulum inevitably swings back and forth, the practical reality is that we will never recreate that particular set of circumstances. A global economy has made us more transient than ever. Moreover, there are many minority groups – women, African-Americans and other non-white ethnic groups, and homosexuals – whose plight has been ignored in that rosy picture of the past. The challenge is to remember the community's ability to muster informal social control and create new ways to tap into and reinvent that power today.

Rebuilding Informal Social Control

Community policing broadens the police mandate beyond formal social control – enforcement of the law – to include working with the community to reinvigorate and rebuild informal social control through community building and community-based problem solving. Much of the confusion about community policing's ill-deserved reputation as being soft on crime stems from asking police to look beyond the narrow role of arrest in solving crime problems. Community policing requires addressing the underlying dynamics that allow crime and disorder to gain a toehold and flourish, and this is misunderstood as ignoring serious crime.

If we think of a young boy who bullies and kicks a younger child or steals something from a neighborhood store, there was a time within memory when the odds were that other parents and adults in the neighborhood would intervene directly and march the youngster home to his parents (and the parents would believe their neighbors' version of what happened). Today, however, it is more likely that the adult would call the police, substituting an expensive and less powerful system for community and family control. Yet if we do not find more effective ways of intervening to resolve problems in which youths are involved, too many grow up to commit adult crimes. So is it soft on crime to involve police in efforts to build community, as a means of reinventing that sense of shared responsibility? Only if you take the narrowest view.

Bruce Benson, Director of Public Safety at Michigan State University, reminds us that we have few solutions to reform the hardened 30-year-old criminal. "If we want to make our communities safer over time, we have to find ways of doing a better job of intervening with our 10- and 12-year-olds." Ironically, of course, it is so-called "petty" crimes, the ones most likely to be committed by juveniles, that receive less attention.

In an elegant analysis of priorities, Canada's Chris Braiden compared bank robberies and bicycle thefts. In the macho world of policing, officers who rush to the scene of a bank robbery are viewed as doing serious police work. Investigating a bicycle theft pales in comparison. Yet Braiden compared the money lost to both kinds of theft in Canada each year and discovered that the ratio was roughly five or six dollars to one in favor of bicycles.

Those bicycle thefts also directly affect far more people. (Citizens rarely, if ever, suffer a direct loss when a bank is robbed, but many must pay out of pocket to replace the bike.) And bank robberies are committed by criminals who are hard to redeem, while the bicycle is often stolen by a youngster who may well get the wrong message if no one seems to care.

Braiden is not arguing that the police should do less in response to bank robberies, but that long-term solutions to crime problems require doing more about the bicycle thefts. The officer who engages the community in creative solutions to petty crime plays an equally valid role in dealing with serious crime as the officer responding to the bank robbery, and departments must do more to acknowledge the importance of such efforts.

Community policing offers a philosophy that embraces involving the community in reaching out to kids. In a suburb of Toronto, an officer fielded a call from a man who was concerned that a group of kids from a low-income housing development many blocks away was playing ball in front of his house. The man said the kids obviously did not live there (he could tell by their shabby clothes) and that he was worried that they were casing the neighborhood. The officer persuaded the man to go out and talk with the kids, to ask them why they had chosen to play in this neighborhood.

A couple hours later, the man called back to say that he had discovered the kids had no safe place to play in their own neighborhood. In fact, the man was so captivated with the youngsters that he agreed to be their coach and find them a place to play.

Of course, such heart-warming anecdotes can always be counterbalanced by those cases where a good Samaritan intervenes and is attacked as a result. Yet community policing rests on the belief that the community must shoulder its fair share of the responsibility – and risk – for rebuilding that all-important sense of community. The challenge becomes how to get the community involved.

Building Civic and Community Support

If community policing is to succeed, it must enlist the support of both geographic communities and communities of interest – all of the groups in the Big Six. As mentioned earlier, two theories are relevant to community policing: *normative sponsorship theory* and *critical social theory*. They provide a framework that allows us to see how various groups within the community can be brought on board.

While an oversimplification, critical social theory proposes that people will behave in accordance with their own enlightened self-interest, once they see what that is. First, people need information to understand their condition (enlightenment). Then they can take action (empowerment) to improve their condition, and success (emancipation) leads to liberation through this combination of reflection and social action.

Normative sponsorship theory proposes that a community effort will only be "sponsored" (supported) if it is normative (within the limits of the established standards of the community) to all persons and interest groups involved. Without a serious common problem, we often see competing interest groups pulling apart. Any threat to life, livelihood, and liberty would obviously rise to the level that could encourage competing groups to set their differences aside. Moreover, each group must be able to justify, and hence legitimize, the common group goal within its own pattern of attitudes, values, norms, and goals.

The more that those attitudes, values, norms and goals of the participating groups converge, the easier it is for them to agree upon common goals. [The participating groups, however, do not necessarily have to justify their involvement in or acceptance of a group goal (Sower, 1957).] In other words,

- for a community to begin any new effort, the effort itself must reflect the community's basic standards;

- for the community to come together to start this new effort, at least two of the major groups in the community must agree that the project is worth doing and that it is consistent with their attitudes, values, norms, and goals; and

- the more that the groups willing to take this leadership role have in common, the more that they can agree on common goals, while recognizing that subsequent groups that sign on to help may not have the same reasons for coming on board.

While the benefits of implementing community policing to strengthen informal social control seem obvious, there are undeniable difficulties involved in recruiting the participation and support of specific groups. What's in it for each of the Big Six and how does the community policing philosophy converge or conflict with their values?

What's in It for Police?

If we start with the first of the Big Six, the police department, it is fair to ask why they would attempt such a difficult reform. The surge in interest in community policing began in the mid-1980s, when the invention of crack cocaine spawned a surge of violence first in urban "hot spots" and then beyond. Prior to that, community policing was an intriguing and promising experiment, but the emergence of crack-fueled violence propelled community policing into more and more police agencies for two main reasons: (1) the existing system proved incapable of dealing with the crack epidemic and (2) money became available to make the change.

At first, there was great enthusiasm within law enforcement for the much-ballyhooed war on drugs. The logic seemed obvious – arrest all the bad guys and drug violence would disappear. But soon it became evident that investing in more of the same – heavy-handed sweeps and crackdowns – did little more than clog jails and prisons without making the streets safer. In fact, it often seemed that the dealers were back on the street faster than the arresting officers. Even when the police succeeded in putting dealers behind bars, there was always a fresh crop of new dealers willing to take their place – and, in many cases, willing to murder their way in. This was clearly a case where the answer was not to work harder but smarter.

As funding from the U.S. Department of Housing and Urban Affairs and then through the Crime Act of 1994 provided the money to make the transition, as well as the training and technical assistance to do so, many police departments had good reason to adopt this new approach. Of course, departments eager to qualify for the new funds often pretended to know more about community policing than they actually did. But the incentive was there, especially as community policing's successes prompted more and more departments to jump on the bandwagon.

The payoff for police is also, very simply, that, given half a chance, community policing works. The power of partnership and collaboration is such that even when mistakes are made, community policing often triumphs.

What's in It for Residents?

Those who live in high-crime/high-disorder neighborhoods are clear winners under community policing for many reasons. First and foremost, community policing offers new strategies to solve the problems that people in troubled and dangerous neighborhoods care about most. Moreover, it does so by empowering citizens and treating them with respect as equal partners in identifying, prioritizing, and solving problems. As Police Executive Research Forum senior researcher Drew Diamond discussed in his article "Policing from the Perimeter" (n.d.), low-income/high-crime neighborhoods have traditionally been underserved compared to the amount of crime and disorder they suffer. The community policing principle of equity promises that they will receive the level of service needed to deal with their problems.

It should be noted, however, that restructuring the department so that police can spend more time in high-crime neighborhoods implies reductions in service elsewhere, logically to the more affluent (and more powerful) constituents. The challenge for departments is to mount a credible case that it is in the enlightened self-interest of middle- and upper-class voters and taxpayers to support community policing. Mounting an appeal to altruism is noble, but it is also a harder sell than a clear example of how it directly benefits them.

So what's in it for people who live in relatively safe neighborhoods? Why is it in their enlightened self-interest to accept a perceived cut in service? One of the best arguments is that history shows that problems never stay contained. Crack, which found its initial niche in high-crime neighborhoods, inevitably found its way into the hands of teenagers from more affluent communities. Problems with crime and violence have spread, so it is in the enlightened self-interest of people in more affluent neighborhoods to invest in strategies that can help to eliminate these problems.

What's in It for Businesses?

The same basic arguments hold true for business. It is easier to persuade the owner of the mom-and-pop store in a high-crime neighborhood to support community policing than to convince the corporation whose headquarters and factories are miles away, behind fences patrolled by security guards. The hardest sell of all may be retail stores that have traditionally benefited from police patrols that are then cut to provide officers time for community building and problem solving in residential areas. Again, altruism is less persuasive than self-interest, so the key lies in making the case that problems left unchecked in one area eventually become everyone's problem. Community policing also means that police will work smarter on the problems that businesses face.

What's in It for Civic Officials?

Public administrators have long undervalued direct citizen participation, which they often view as amateurish and ill-informed. Indeed, public officials often think that involving citizens merely increases the likelihood of dissension and delay, unless they can be counted on to act as a rubber stamp. Community policing therefore faced an uphill battle in persuading civic officials that the change was worth the effort.

Again, it was the explosion of violence associated with the emergence of the crack trade in the mid-1980s that made the case for community policing for one reason – it was clear that the existing system was failing. Nothing captures the attention of elected officials more than unhappy constituents demanding change. As community policing experiments began to demonstrate the ability to reduce open drug dealing, a growing sense of dread and desperation helped to bring normally risk-averse politicians on board.

The danger for politicians, however, is that community policing can provide an alternative opportunity for citizens seeking redress. The voter who wants something done about the potholes in front of his or her house or the unreliable garbage pickup may work through his or her local police officer rather than turning to an elected official. In that sense, community policing can threaten a politician's base of support. One of the more effective solutions is for the police to share credit with the politicians whenever possible, so that the change clearly benefits them.

What about Other Agencies, Institutions, and Non-Profit Groups?

Finding the key to bringing these agencies on board involves persuading them that community policing helps them with their jobs. Middle- and high-school administrators, for example, have good reason to support community policing when it offers them direct help with chronic problems such as truancy. Non-profit agencies benefit when they have the chance to become part of a problem-solving team that ensures their needs are not ignored. Admittedly, the sanitation department held accountable for the uncollected garbage in the previous example may not be delighted to find yet another civil servant monitoring their performance, but the challenge to the department is to find ways to enlist and maintain their support. Perhaps the most potent appeals are that a collaborative community policing approach works, and it spreads the workload among more agencies, thereby easing the load on all.

Developing Community Involvement

Identifying community policing's potential benefits to various groups is only one-half of the battle. The next challenge is to use those persuasive arguments to bring them to the table, so that groups can collaborate on community building and community-based problem solving. Again, the challenges and opportunities are different for different groups.

Enlisting the participation and support of civic officials, non-profit groups, institutions such as churches and schools, and public agencies often requires recruiting individual champions within the organization one by one. It would be naïve to suppose that the entire city council will immediately see the wisdom of working as partners with the police and the community in new ways. But odds are that there is one person on the council willing to try.

Community policing also increases the number of "recruiters" within the department, by empowering officers at all levels to reach out for help. In the past, only the chief and top command had the authority to approach top officials and executives. Community policing freed Officer Wayne Barton of Boca Raton, Florida, who succeeded in securing a pledge of more than $250,000 from the Zale's jewelry corporation to pay for the college education of kids in his public housing beat.

One common oversight, however, is the failure to document key people. If an officer identifies the one person in code enforcement who is willing to cut red tape, that name should be documented and shared. It can be a temptation to keep the individual as a personal secret, particularly since sharing the name could mean having to wait in line the next time, but the department suffers when officers keep their own lists of helpers that they are unwilling to share.

Some communities are experimenting with decentralized facilities where police share space with representatives of other groups that can help – what Trojanowicz called the "Neighborhood Network Center" concept. This allows increased opportunities for formal and informal sharing of information, and it also allows pooling and sharing scarce resources. Ideally, if the problem is a troubled youth, the police officer could assemble a team of professionals that could investigate and intervene. Troubled kids often come from families with multiple problems, so the team roster might eventually include a school counselor, social worker, a drug counselor, and maybe even a code enforcement official to make the landlord abide by the terms of the lease.

The virtue of having a number of professionals in the same office back into the community is obvious, but the danger is that they end up spending more time talking to each other than reaching out to the community. Supervisors must be alert to that danger and quickly take steps to ensure that the professionals focus on outreach and include the community in their teams and partnerships.

Tips on Grass-Roots Organizing

In the case of community residents, overcoming apathy is no easy task, and sustaining momentum can be even more difficult. Many department host a series of town hall meetings as part of initial implementation of community policing, as a means of setting a new tone of openness and equality. Here again, active listening is part of the key. If police arrive with the attitude that they are the experts with all the answers, it does not send the message that they are ready to collaborate as partners. The approach instead should be, "We're here to listen; tell us your concerns and your ideas."

Time and again, police discover that the problems that they thought would be the community's main concerns – the most serious crimes of murder, rape, robbery, and assault – are not at the top of the list. Idle teens on the street; low-level drug dealing; open drinking in the park; abandoned buildings; panhandlers, prostitutes, and runaways – these are often the issues that make residents fear that the neighborhood is headed downhill. However, the challenge eventually becomes enlisting participation and support neighborhood by neighborhood.

The goal then becomes involving residents in collaborative efforts to prioritize and solve the problems that they care about most. Yet a frustrated officer in a training session echoed a common problem, "I have tried everything I can think of and I still can't get more than a handful of people to a community meeting." Some ideas:

- **Whose Agenda Is It?/Start Small** – When asked about his efforts, the officer above talked about how he had tried to hold a series of meetings to deal with drug problems in their public housing development. The problem was, of course, that this was his goal and not theirs. He had not yet done anything to earn their trust, and yet he was asking them to stick their necks out far enough to become targets for the drug dealers. Obviously that was asking far too much as a first step. A far more modest goal focused on community building first might make better sense.

- **Get the Kids and Adults Will Follow** – Adults, particularly those who have had negative experiences with police, can be understandably wary of officers who insist, "We're from the government and we're here to help – trust us." Kids, on the other hand, with their combination of curiosity and candor, are often more willing to give officers a chance. Organize a soccer league. Invite kids to videotape a documentary about the neighborhood and then air it on public access television. Work with the local library on a summer reading program. Develop a mentoring program in partnership with the local faith community. Earn and maintain the trust of the young people and the adults will not be far behind.

- **Hold Meetings with the Community in Mind** – If you want people to attend, you must make the meetings inviting and appealing. Some considerations:

  - **Location** – Is the facility convenient and accessible, including to the disabled?

  - **Time of Day/Day of Week** – Are these convenient for the majority of the community (or for the officers)?

  - **Transportation** – In low-income neighborhoods, it may be especially important to provide free transportation. A failure to do so may particularly impact the participation of older residents, who often have the potential to become community policing's staunchest supporters.

  - **Security** – Do residents feel safe both arriving and leaving? Would it make sense to organize an escort service or a buddy system?

  - **Child Care** – Going the extra distance to recruit volunteers to mind the children not only increases participation, but it often means fewer interruptions during meetings.

  - **Refreshments** – No budget? Find sponsors.

  - **Door Prizes** – This is one way to go the extra mile to encourage participation.

- **Pre-Planning** – Invite two or three informal leaders in the community to help you troubleshoot plans for the meeting. Not only does this secure their buy-in but also their best thinking. What are the barriers and obstacles? Are there issues of language and diversity that should be explored? Are there animosities, divisions, or conflicts within the community that could jeopardize participation? What other things would attract people to come? What are turnoffs?

- **Publicity** – Allow enough advance time and then strategize to maximize reinforcement. In advertising, the rule of thumb is that it requires at least three exposures to the message to overcome sales resistance. Make sure that residents see at least three mentions of the meeting – on flyers; in newsletters; in announcements at their church, synagogue, or mosque; in the newspaper; and on the local radio station's community calendar.

- **Publish the Agenda** – People like to know what they are getting into. Make sure that the agenda revolves around their concerns and not just police priorities.

- **Bring a Friend** – Buttonhole individuals you know and urge them to bring a new friend to the meeting, someone who has not been there before.

- **Telephone Tree** – Organize a telephone tree, where one person calls three or four specified people on their list, and they each call three or four specified people on their list. Have the calls take place no more than a day or two before the meeting as a last-minute reminder.

- **Offer Variety** – An occasional speaker might be one possibility. Use a video clip to stimulate discussion. Invite residents from other neighborhoods with similar problems.

If that sounds like more work than you had anticipated, remember that the alternative is enduring the embarrassment and frustration of a low turnout. Moreover, these meetings are often just the beginning. The goal in part is to identify community members whose help will be essential in working with others to solve specific problems. Setting up subsequent problem-solving sessions with a broad cross-section of individuals who exhibit a wide range of income, educational levels, social status, and life experience can present even more daunting challenges.

Maintaining Momentum

While nothing succeeds like success, one of the biggest problems that police face is that participation tends to decline as threats decrease. The community comes together with great fervor to confront the dealers on the street, and then when they disappear (or move elsewhere), where is the urgency to attend the next meeting?

On the one hand, it is unreasonable to expect the intensity to remain at fever pitch. Yet it is also sheer folly to allow gains to slip away. As the example above illustrates, the reality of displacement means that communities that are organized may not be able to prevent all crime from occurring, but they can reduce the likelihood that it will occur in their neighborhood. Once they lose that cohesion, however, they risk becoming a target again.

Part of the answer is to develop long-range plans to sustain momentum. Host problem-solving sessions on how to maintain involvement and support, and how to recruit new members for those who inevitably fall away. Approach inertia with the same tactics and techniques that you would use to confront any other serious problem in the community.

Questions and Answers

How can the department enlist the support of the Big Six? Remember that each group – police departments, communities, elected civic officials, business communities, public and non-profit agencies, and the media – has its own agenda and interests, so any appeal for participation must resonate within the context of their wants and needs. Approach enlisting their participation as you would any other problem – brainstorm, experiment, and be prepared to keep trying.

How does a community policing officer get input from the community to know what their concerns are? Face-to-face contact is still the best way for people to share information. Regular meetings with the community can help to build trust and encourage honesty and candor. Surveys can augment open-ended community sessions, but survey participation tends to fall off sharply in low-income neighborhoods. Written surveys, for example, automatically exclude the illiterate. Telephone surveys ignore those too poor to have a phone. Even door-to-door surveys miss those who are not home. If you want to know what people really think, you must get together with them and listen.

Why doesn't the threat of crime and drug problems encourage greater community participation? Fear of crime can be as big a problem as crime itself, since it keeps people trapped in their homes. What appears to be apathy may actually be resignation and exhaustion. Involving the community, particularly in areas where residents have routinely been marginalized and ignored, is a long-term process. Go back to the checklist above that offers ideas on how to make meetings inviting and accessible and keep trying.

Why should citizens identify the problems? The citizens are in the best position to know what is needed in their neighborhoods. They also know what is best for them. Ask for their input, listen to them, and you stand a much better chance of enlisting their direct participation and support. They will have a stake in both the process and the outcome.

Why does community policing emphasize getting information from law-abiding citizens? The two groups of people who have information that can prevent and solve crime are criminals and their law-abiding families, friends, and neighbors. Prior to community policing, departments spent most of their time trying to get information about crime from the "bad guys," the ones with the most to lose. Community policing recognizes that information is the lifeblood of policing, and strategies that involve citizens as the eyes and ears of the police make sense. Community policing promotes trust between people and their police, which encourages people to tell what they know. Outreach into the community provides new informal opportunities for people to share what they know without singling themselves out for retribution.

How does community policing provide a hedge against vigilantism? Citizens in problem neighborhoods are often frustrated by the amount of crime and disorder they endure. They can lose confidence in the criminal justice system, which fosters the impulse to take the law into their own hands. Community policing offers hope that something will be done, with their help. Officers in the community can tap the energy of the people and direct it into positive action instead.

Should the police department initiate community policing and then involve the community, or should the community be involved from the beginning? The community must be involved from the beginning, including the planning process. Public forums, focus groups, surveys, small-group meetings, and other methods for obtaining citizen input are critical to setting the tone for the long term.

How can police overcome apathy and maintain momentum? People are often apathetic unless or until high-visibility crimes (murder, rape, robbery) occur in their neighborhoods. Unfortunately, once a particular problem is dealt with, it is often difficult to keep the community "fired up," to continue working on problems so that they do not occur again. That is why it is important to identify local leaders – the go-getters who are willing to continue problem-solving even without a current crisis. Citizens need to understand that dealing with the symptoms is not enough. Attaining long-term goals requires continuous commitment. Communities need to be made safer not just for the present but for the future.

Some people are reluctant to get involved because of a fear of retaliation from criminals. How does community policing address this? There is strength in numbers. When people see that they are not alone in identifying and solving problems, they become more confident and therefore more active. The police must also be part of the solution, working with the community on creating ways to keep residents safe.

What is a realistic expectation for citizen involvement? People can make different kinds of contributions, ranging from being a leader who organizes block associations, to being the person at home addressing envelopes for a community newsletter, to those who offer firsthand assistance to projects. Not all citizens will be actively involved. Once positive change happens, often more people will get involved.

How do you deal with self-proclaimed community leaders who may not represent anyone but themselves? Policing is dependent upon the cooperation of the community. However, in some cases, there are persons who call themselves community leaders who may not be. Sadly as well, they may actually be divisive and destructive of efforts to solve problems. The challenge is to handle these potentially explosive situations with respect and tact. The best bet is to involve other community members who can help defuse or resolve the situation, and the best answers require a case-by-case approach.

SECTION V
Issues in Hiring and Training

Attracting and Hiring the Right Officers

The color of the actual collar may still be blue, but policing has become a white-collar profession, whose ranks are increasingly filled by people with college degrees. The beat cop at the turn of the twentieth century was hired more for his muscle and his ability to pound the pavement than for his communication and problem-solving skills. In contrast, as we approach the turn of the twenty-first century, we no longer see policing as physical work. Now entry-level officers operate as mini-chiefs in the community.

Among the questions that this section will address are: What do police agencies want and need in new recruits? Where can they find good candidates, and how can they attract them when they do? Then we will look at training.

Identifying Attributes and Skills

The line can easily blur when trying to differentiate between the skills that a good recruit should already possess and those that can be inculcated or enhanced by training later. Of course, there are certain baseline abilities that a candidate must possess, ranging from sufficient physical strength and stamina for the job to a personal commitment to integrity and honesty. However, community policing emphasizes the need for officers with superior community and interpersonal skills.

Communication

Police officers have always needed good verbal skills for interviewing, as well as writing skills sufficient to produce coherent, useful, and complete reports. Clearly as well, the best officers have always been students of human nature, capable of assessing a wide variety of situations quickly.

Community policing ups the ante even further. The ideal candidate must be able to talk with people from a wide array of backgrounds, as equal partners, not as the authoritarian cop who must be obeyed. Candidates must be able to interact as easily with the panhandler on the street as with the bank vice-president or school superintendent. Not only must the officer be able to communicate face-to-face, the ideal candidate should also have the skills to chair a meeting. Training can indeed help in that regard, but the basic skills must be there on which to build.

The bar is also higher for written communication skills. For one thing, even a cursory review of officer reports often uncovers too many errors and omissions. If a department is to move to a more sophisticated level of problem solving, it cannot accept a standard that allows "garbage in/garbage out." Police increasingly find themselves working on collaborative efforts that require writing reports for individuals and groups outside the agency. The job can also include writing articles and notices for newsletters.

Interpersonal Skills

Dealing with Diversity

Given the diversity within police agencies and in the community, candidates must exhibit tolerance, respect, and sensitivity to others. Elsie Scott, former head of training for the New York City Police Department and past executive director of the National Organization of Black Law Enforcement Executives, said that departments must do their best to attract candidates who are free of bias. "The problem with prejudice is that it often comes out under stress, and police work is stressful," she said.

Police agencies have come a long way since the days when they were the exclusive bastions of white males. Women and minorities still are not at parity, and there are always concerns about the "glass ceiling," but obvious progress continues to be made. Gone are the days when the total number of minority or female chiefs could have held their meetings in a phone booth. Even a decade ago, for example, there was little, if any, open acknowledgment of gay police officers, and now a growing number of departments respect their contribution.

Education about diversity can help everyone understand cultural attributes of various groups, particularly those with which they may have had limited exposure. However, the training works best when it builds on basic attitudes of equity and fair play.

Collaboration and Creativity

Collaboration requires employing superior communication skills in service of forging working partnerships. The ideal candidate for police work today should already possess the ability to work as part of a team. The old paradigm stressed a willingness to take orders, and then to give them. Community policing requires personnel that can collaborate as equal partners, regardless of rank or status. The best candidates are those who are self-starters, eager to try new ideas to solve the problem, rather than individuals who wait to be told by superiors precisely what to do.

Conflict Resolution/Crisis Intervention

Training can indeed enhance these interpersonal skills, but again, candidates who understand the need to use a wide variety of approaches to situations are more likely to benefit from training that offers new tips and ideas. The best police officers have always been willing and able to talk themselves and others out of trouble. There simply cannot always be a one-size-fits-all response to all situations, and a tactical retreat may sometimes be far preferable to escalating the tensions.

Bringing the Best Aboard

Now that we have a clearer picture of the ideal candidates for a community policing department, where is the best place to look for them? Recruiters have often focused on criminal justice majors and individuals with at least some military training, yet that can unduly narrow the pool. Indeed, there are those who question whether the military's focus on obedience makes that experience the best predictor of success in a community policing department that emphasizes autonomy and creativity.

The skills outlined above as ideal are clearly in the line with those required to be a good teacher, social worker, or perhaps a nurse, and recruiting recent graduates from those disciplines can assist in bringing greater diversity to the department. Without becoming embroiled in the contentious debate about affirmative action, the fact remains that the face of the police department must reflect a cross-section of the community to maintain credibility and respect. Individuals of different experience enhance the ability of the department to consider a wider array of opinions and perspectives.

The issue of where to look for the best candidates raises the controversial issue of residency. Should police be required to live in the communities they serve? All too often, agencies that require that their officers live in the city simply end up with a significant number of officers who lie about where they reside. A number of cities have taken a more creative approach, offering police officers attractive terms to lure them into buying a house within the jurisdiction, particularly in low-income neighborhoods. Packages often include a reduced sale price, no down payment, low or zero interest, or some combination of such terms. These opportunities can be particularly inviting to young officers who might otherwise not be able to afford their own homes. There is little doubt that police officers who have a personal stake and family stake in the safety of the jurisdiction have even greater incentive to do a good job, the issue is how best to encourage them to live where they work.

What does it take for a department to attract the best of the best? Never underestimate the importance of pay – but do not overestimate it either. A sheriff's department in Texas may not pay a beginning officer more than $15,000 a year. Meanwhile, in places such as Suffolk County on Long Island in New York, routinely listed as one of the highest-paying departments in the country, entry-level officers can make at least three times as much. Even though living expenses are significantly higher near New York City than in a small town in Texas, quality policing deserves quality pay.

However, people want more than financial compensation; the people who go into police work want a job that allows them to make a difference. It is therefore worth mentioning again that community policing enhances job satisfaction through job enhancement (more freedom, flexibility, autonomy, creativity) and job enlargement (more responsibility and authority). When appealing to college students in the School of Education at the local university, there is no doubt that many of them will never have thought of policing as a field that would allow them to use their talents. Many of the best candidates self-select out of the field, because the image of police officers that they grew up with on TV and in the movies feeds into the action myth that the job is all about sirens and gunplay. Young people who want to help make this a better world need to be told face-to-face to think about policing as a career, even if they have never done so before.

Developing a Comprehensive Training Strategy

A change as profound as community policing requires developing a comprehensive training strategy, one that not only reaches everyone in the police department, sworn, non-sworn, and civilian, but which also includes input from and participation of the community. It must provide skills and tools for everyone from the inexperienced rookie to the seasoned veteran. The community policing training strategy must also provide opportunities for reinforcement over time, as new needs emerge.

This section will explore how community policing training should be delivered and what it should cover. It will also include an analysis of specific issues related to the different kinds of training that police receive – academy, field training, in-service. The section concludes with a discussion of the importance of inventing new initiatives to provide leadership training to the community.

How to Train – Andragogy versus Pedagogy

Before identifying what should be taught, it pays to discuss how to teach community policing, including the issue of how best to teach adults. *Andragogy* refers to the teaching of adults, and *pedagogy* refers to the teaching of children. Research confirms that the pedagogical model that many of us grew up with – crowded lectures given by teachers, with us taking notes – simply does not work as well as interactive and experiential learning.

Adult learning theory explains that people learn best when they are challenged to teach themselves – through discovery, invention, brainstorming, and teamwork. As we will see, trainers must work hard to translate the teaching points into exercises, scenarios, role plays, and interactive discussions, augmented with mini-lectures peppered with visual aids. In keeping with the community policing philosophy, training becomes an exercise in partnership rather than experts instructing the ignorant. When in doubt, always remember that people would rather listen to themselves than to you.

Teaching adults also means remembering their special needs. Allow more frequent breaks, since adults tire more easily. Use larger print so that aging participants do not need to strain their eyes to read. The following chart identifies some of the basic differences between teaching children and adults, and it leaves space for you to add your own notes.

FACETS OF LEARNING

CHILDREN	ADULTS
Young & uninformed	Older & experienced
Blank slate	Body of knowledge
Naïve & accepting	Sophisticated & inquisitive
Open to new ideas	Demand relevance
Short attention span	More focused
Energetic	Tire more easily
Information isolated	Connect information to knowledge & experience
_____	_____
_____	_____
_____	_____

Source: Originally created by Bonnie Bucqueroux for the National Organization of Black Law Enforcement Executives and the Community Policing Consortium.

Among the items above that deserve special mention is the reference that adults are sophisticated and quicker to question. Good trainers know that they will lose their credibility if the audience detects any hint of pretense or phoniness. If police, in particular, discover that something in the material simply does not make sense or rings false, the entire training curriculum may be called into question. Trainers of police are much better off asking the participants for their own thoughts on an issue, and then discussing it, than they are trying to pass off their thoughts to the participants.

Important as well is that adults learn by connecting the new information to their experience. Theories and principles are important, but the goal is to tie them to specific, real-life examples, and, again, the best experts are the police themselves. Training should always go from the general to the specific, not the specific to the general.

Much of police training, of necessity, has focused on building specific law enforcement skills and techniques: firearms training, interviewing and investigative techniques, report writing, appropriate use of force, driving (pursuit), first-aid. As this suggests, much of the training is therefore action-oriented, focused, and specific.

As a result, the first impulse in developing training in community policing is likely to be to make this yet another discrete unit – a specific number of hours devoted to community policing as a stand-alone topic. There are indeed six specific content areas that community policing training must address (see below), and it may make sense to offer specific instruction on these topics. However, the real challenge lies in finding ways to integrate and infuse the community policing philosophy into all aspects of training, and that may well look different in different contexts.

What Should Police Be Taught?

There are six basic content areas that a comprehensive community policing curriculum must cover. Various curricula may mix, match, blend, and overlap, but all should at least address:

- **What Is Community Policing?** – At a minimum, training participants must receive a workable definition of community policing, based on the foundation of the Ten Principles. Equally important is that participants understand how adopting the community policing philosophy will change the way that the department operates and how it will impact their specific role in the organization.

- **Leadership** – Community policing asks everyone in the department to exhibit leadership, at all levels and positions. Training must translate that goal into strategies and ideas that people can use.

- **Community Building and Problem Solving** – These two cornerstones of police activity require particular care and attention and constant updating and reinforcement. Along with leadership training, training that focuses on community building and problem solving can be used to deal with any emerging concern. Whether the problem at hand is illegal drugs or violence against women, bringing leadership, community building, and problem solving to bear on the issue is what community policing is all about.

- **Diversity** – In retrospect, it seems that teaching diversity as a separate discipline tends to marginalize and compartmentalize issues that should be integrated into everything that police do. The goal should be to weave strategies to enhance tolerance, respect, and compassion into every aspect of police training, in the same way that the community policing philosophy must infuse the entire curriculum.

- **Skill Building** – The hiring section above identified communication and interpersonal skills that become even more important with community policing. In some cases, it may make sense to offer specific instruction on verbal and writing skills, for example. Yet all training must capitalize on opportunities to provide participants with coaching and tips on how they can improve performance. Training on other issues can intentionally structure opportunities for participants to hone specific skills. For example, trainers can include opportunities for participants to practice their public speaking skills, by encouraging teams to rotate the assignment of the spokesperson who reports out to the larger group so that everyone, even the shyest, gets a chance. As this suggests, the challenge is to think through every element of the training, to ensure that each moment carries as much freight as possible.

Tips on Enhancing Interactivity

It cannot be stressed enough that effective training requires more than offering lectures and "war stories" (though both can have their place). In many ways, the best training allows people to work together to discover the wisdom that they already know. Turning training into a collaborative enterprise models the behavior that community policing requires. The following is offered both as a yardstick against which to measure the training options available, and as a blueprint for improving your own training sessions.

- **Mini-Lectures** – There are instances where specific information, usually technical information or theory, is best delivered by brief bursts of lecture. Yet lecture should also be built around discussion with the audience, inviting them to answer and ask questions. These mini-lectures benefit from support from visual aids – overheads; presentation programs such as PowerPoint; and video clips. Interactivity is also enhanced by including mini-tests or surveys, including those that can be repeated to identify changes in thinking.

- **Role Plays** – A role play offers a realistic slice of life that can then be dissected to illustrate various real-life situations that dramatize specific issues and concerns. For example, if the training is aimed at instructing middle managers about their role in providing leadership for community policing, a role play built around common themes of resistance would make sense. For example:

  - Someone plays the crusty sergeant who heckles the trainer from the back of the room, as the trainer talks about forming partnerships with the community.

  - Re-run that same scenario changing the gender and race of the participants.

  - Devote the next 10 to 15 minutes to de-briefing the audience through a series of structured questions about the issues. Where does resistance come from? What is the best way to handle the situation? How do the dynamics change as the attributes of the participants change?

  There can be times when enlisting actors makes sense, but on most occasions, effective role plays rely on volunteers who are willing to participate. Role plays need not last more than three to five minutes, since the bulk of the illumination comes from the structured de-briefing afterward. *Fishbowl role plays* occur in front of the audience of participants, who are then invited to dissect and discuss what they saw. *Multiple role plays* allow a number of different enactments to take place at the same time, with or without observers. The main benefit with multiple role plays all at the same time is that they increase direct participation, and research confirms that people actually retain more when they combine physical movement with intellectual content. That benefit must, however, be balanced against the main drawback, which is that the message may get lost in the confusion.

- **Scenarios** – Scenarios serve the same function as role plays, by asking the participants to react to real-life situations. Use them in place of role plays when the topic or situation is too challenging or complex for a volunteer to act out. Sprinkling scenarios among the role plays also allows covering more topics in less time, since scenarios do not require as much set-up time.

- **Brainstorming Sessions** – These are freewheeling sessions that get the juices flowing by allowing people to offer ideas from the ridiculous to the sublime without fear of ridicule. Such experiences can be liberating, and they undeniably generate ideas beyond what any one individual sitting alone could achieve.

- **Exercises** – Individual and team exercises range from the generic, which teach basic issues, values, or skills, to the specific, such as problem solving and action planning exercises designed to translate into further action in the real world after the training ends. Generic exercises have merit. A popular training exercise built on a puzzle that can only be solved by going outside the lines has become so well-known that "thinking outside the box" has now become a cliché. Yet it is the exercises built around real problems in the department or in the community and those that challenge participants to begin doing real planning that are likely to have the greatest impact. They provide people an opportunity to test their skills within the context of the safe training environment, where trainers and facilitators can coach them onto the right track.

- **New Media/New Opportunities** – With the advent of interactivity through the Internet and the World Wide Web, we are just beginning to explore this new environment as a unique way to provide training and technical assistance. The last section deals with the possibilities in more detail, but online training and collaborative problem solving may well expand training options into an around-the-clock activity.

Basic Academy Training

It is when entry-level police officers join the organization that they are the most open to adopting a philosophical mind-set for the police role. Even in situations where recruits have prior experience, they are usually willing to consider subtle changes in their role as they enter a new environment. The basic academy setting should offer two intertwining tracks on community policing:

- **"Dedicated" Community Policing Training** – This is training devoted to explaining what community policing is and how it works, including specifics such as the definition and philosophy of community policing, based on the Ten Principles and the vision, values, and mission of the department; effective leadership; community building and problem solving; and specific skill building (including concepts such as verbal judo), all within the context of diversity.

- **Basic Training** - Community policing should be a common thread running through as much of the other training courses as possible, such as:

    - **Patrol Procedures** - Offer strategies for becoming more community oriented and concerned with quality of life and fear of crime issues while on "normal" patrols.

    - **Investigations** - How to engage the community in assisting investigations; directing investigative efforts toward identifying the underlying causes of crime and disorder; encouraging trainees to think more broadly.

    - **Traffic Enforcement and Accident Investigation** - Ideas for diagnosing underlying causes of traffic safety hazards and engaging the community and other service providers in finding resolutions to community traffic safety issues.

    - **Law Enforcement Ethics** - Develop a clear understanding of how community policing must be ground in respect for civil rights and discuss boundaries and opportunities in involving the community. The role of police discretion in using arrest is only one tool of law enforcement. Avoiding the dangers of political and economic corruption when dealing directly with the community.

    - **Arrest Control and Baton and Defensive Tactics** - An underlying philosophical approach to the use of force and physical restraint that includes the principles of the minimum force necessary for humane control; technical proficiency designed to protect officers and citizens alike; and concern for community acceptance of methods.

    - **Policies, Practices, and Procedures** - An understanding of the framework and rules for the delivery of police service and how they support the community policing philosophy, vision, values, and mission.

    - **Community Resources** - Recruits may not have a complete picture of how city services operate. Sessions should emphasize not only the function of various departments and agencies, public and non-profit, but it also makes sense to provide new hires with a full listing of community resources, contact persons, and telephone/fax/E-mail.

Academy training can offer skill building in communications and interpersonal skills, tailored to specific needs. Some jurisdictions have no difficulty in identifying and attracting candidates with exemplary skills, while others would benefit from offering enrichment in areas such as writing and public speaking and conflict resolution/crisis intervention. Departments may want to work with local community colleges or universities, or approach area businesses about having them share their training expertise in these areas.

Other New-Hire Training

When new non-sworn employees are hired into the organization, special attention should be paid to educating them about community policing and how it is their job as well. New employees who have direct contact with the public (dispatchers, report technicians, complaint clerks, records clerks, receptionists, and property and evidence clerks) should be trained in customer service, and all should be introduced to the concepts of community building and problem solving. They should also be trained in understanding how community policing has changed the various roles of officers within the department, including theirs.

The importance of training non-sworn and civilian employees cannot be emphasized enough. Far too often, they feel like second-class citizens. Dispatchers in particular are vitally important to community policing's success. For one thing, they are often a citizen's initial or only contact with the department, and first impressions count. How they explain community policing and police priorities can shape attitude within the community. Their buy-in to the community policing philosophy is essential if we expect them to "sell" it to the consumers of police service.

Police Officer Field Training

How a police officer will act during the early years of his or her career often comes from the experience of field training. Field training may well be the single most crucial element in changing the culture within the department toward a community policing approach. This "OJT/on-the-job" training tends to override whatever trainees learn in college and in the academy, and it often determines where the officer will set boundaries on proper behavior. Mentoring provided by training officers shapes the strategies, techniques, and, most importantly, the role that recruits embrace. This is particularly true when field training is lengthy, and when it involves daily evaluations and feedback to the trainees.

Because of the tremendous impact that field training has on the entire organization, the philosophical orientation and skills of the training officers are crucial. Therefore, training the trainers in community policing is extremely important if they are to transmit that message to others.

Put bluntly, if a field training officer (FTO) does not both believe in and practice the principles of community policing, it will be virtually impossible for rookies – even those who are enthusiastic about community policing – to fulfill their potential. Field training is the crucible in which rookies learn what they need to launch their careers, and trainers who subvert the principles of community policing, whether consciously or because of lack of proper training themselves, can end up undermining community policing's future.

For example, trainers can talk about the virtues of getting out of the patrol car and interacting with the community and working on community problems. But if the rookies do not see them do so with enthusiasm and skill, the training has missed the opportunity to get them started on the right track. Trainers cannot be allowed to slide by with a "do what I say, not what I do" approach.

The job task categories in a structured field training program must be assessed to ensure that they reflect the philosophy and practice of community policing. Bringing these categories into line can require redefinition of performance standards under existing job categories (i.e., field performance, investigation, officer safety, interaction with the public, etc.) or even the devising of new job task categories – with corresponding performance standards – that reflect the community policing philosophy, such as:

- **Knowledge and Application of Resources in Daily Work**

  - An acceptable knowledge base, as reflected in verbal or written tests.

  - Making appropriate referrals on a daily basis.

  - Maintaining a list of appropriate referrals for reference in the field.

  - Taking the time to explain options and resources.

  - Making sure information is correct.

- **Responsiveness to Quality-of-Life Issues in Performance**

  - General recognition of the importance of quality-of-life issues in the community and the need to address them in daily work.

  - Self-initiation of activities such as those listed above.

  - Use of innovative approaches to community building and community-based problem solving.

  - Commitment to the Ten Principles and the vision, values, and mission of the department.

  - Courtesy, empathy, respect, and helpfulness in daily contacts.

  - Focus on solving problems rather than avoiding them or just taking reports.

- **Relationship with the Community**

  - Positive interaction with the community.

  - Face-to-face contact whenever possible.

  - Challenging and empowering citizens to participate in iden-
    tifying and prioritizing problems and in developing short-
    and long-term solutions.

  - Explaining actions and directions to citizens.

  - Following up on citizen questions and concerns.

It is absolutely essential that management closely supervise the field training
program. Weekly evaluations of training officers and sergeants can help
ensure that when someone strays off track from the community policing
model, he or she can be brought back on board quickly. Additionally, field
training sergeants must lead both the trainers and recruits by example during
the daily activities encountered on the street.

In-Service Training

The virtues of in-service training almost go without saying. They provide
existing personnel the education and skills they need to perform to their
fullest in a community policing department. Moreover, this ensures that the
old guard does not undermine these new ideas. In-service training provides
opportunities to build and hone new skills that can carry community policing to the next level. It also plays a crucial role in institutionalizing change
and maintaining momentum.

Workshops on leadership, community building, community-based problem solving, dealing with diversity, addressing special problems (violence
against women, child abuse, drug dealing), and action planning should
include sworn, non-sworn, and civilian personnel and members of the community (which we will discuss in more detail later). As noted previously, a
problem-solving effort that includes a hospital administrator will likely
include strategies involving hospitals, which means that the more points of
view included, the better the solutions and outcomes.

Also valuable is executive leadership training on maximizing community
policing's potential. There may be a need for special sessions on empowering supervisory personnel. The department might consider a series of brown-
bag lunches on topics such as risk-taking and innovation, perhaps with speakers from area corporations.

Finding Effective Training and Technical Assistance

The Crime Act of 1994 established the U.S. Department of Justice's Office of Community-Oriented Police Services (COPS) and the outreach training and technical assistance arm, the Community Policing Consortium, which is made up of major police organizations:

- The International Association of Chiefs of Police (IACP);

- National Organization of Black Law Enforcement Executives (NOBLE);

- National Sheriffs' Association (NSA);

- Police Executive Research Forum (PERF); and

- The Police Foundation.

Offering training and technical assistance to those who receive COPS funding has had a tremendous impact on the quantity and quality of community policing training available. The federal initiative is now expanding the number of Regional Community Policing Institutes. The training available covers a wide range of topics, and the system can accommodate some special needs.

The participating organizations in the consortium also continue to provide their own "brand-name" training based on their particular missions. There are also consultants and trainers nationwide with specific expertise on which departments rely. Word of mouth and references should help narrow the field for departments that want more than what is freely available.

Building a Library

The explosion of information on community policing makes it difficult to stay current, so departments should consider establishing a mini-library, with lending privileges. A catalogue of the articles, research, video and audio tapes, and books could be posted around the department and on the agency's Web site. (It also makes sense to share bookmarks of other Web sites that offer information on community policing.)

If we move beyond the basics, it might make sense to encourage officers to study:

- foreign languages;

- child psychology and development;

- basic psychology;

- political science;

- human relations;

- urban planning;

- gerontology; and

- city management.

The department library could offer books on such topics, since these areas are beyond the scope and the budget of department training.

The challenge requires balancing traditional and non-traditional training and ensuring that the community policing philosophy infuses both. If all the worthwhile skills cannot be added to basic training, there may be ways to provide them in advanced training or through self-paced studies, by assigning trainers to roll call, or by providing training through new technologies like video and audio cassettes, and the Internet and CD-ROMs.

Who Trains the Community?

Many times, training for the community is limited to citizen academies and ride-alongs. While such efforts help educate the community about police work, they pale in comparison to involving the police and a broad range of community leaders in training together in leadership, community building, and problem solving. Unfortunately, however, there are often barriers that prevent joint training: restrictions on use of funds; problems in scheduling; and short time horizons. In truth, one of the major hurdles is often that police express their reluctance to bring citizens to the training.

Yet anybody who has seen firsthand the remarkable synergy that occurs when police and community come together to brainstorm about real problems knows that more must be done to cut red tape and overcome hesitation. This is the kind of training that produces concrete plans that address real problems in the community. Such efforts also build the partnerships that serve as the foundation for long-term momentum.

The goal should be to do more to provide the community the training they need to fulfill their role as equal partners in the process of making their neighborhoods safer. The police have the U.S. Department of Justice for training assistance, and local agencies often have their own training and enrichment programs. Where can average citizens and informal and formal community leaders turn for help?

Michigan State University professor and author Carl S. Taylor, who was mentored early in his career by Robert Trojanowicz, argues that training should now focus as much on the community as on police. "We have reached a point in the evolution of our understanding about the power of the community to reduce and control violence to recognize the urgency of providing grass-roots training in community leadership."

Taylor, a nationally renowned expert in community violence, is launching a new initiative, the Center for Community Leadership, which he plans to use to help fill the current gap in training for the community. "Trojanowicz always said that until we are all safe, no one is safe," said Taylor. "We believe that only when the community learns how to exercise its power to enhance public safety will we be able to fulfill that promise."

Questions and Answers

Is training the key in implementing and institutionalizing community policing? It would be hard to undervalue the power of training to support short- and long-term change. But it would also be a mistake to think that training can substitute for good management and consistent leadership at all levels. Training in leadership is community policing's best hope now and for the future.

What is the ideal training for patrol officers so that they learn community building and community-based problem solving? The goal should be to think of training as a continuous process that never stops, and then to tailor what this means for any specific police agency through the prism of their resources, limitations, and opportunities. In addition to workshops and training sessions on the tactics and techniques of community building and problem solving, departments could do more to reinforce that training with support in the field. Send someone designated as a training coach into the field to accompany officers to meetings and provide insights, suggestions, and ideas. Be creative in using the Internet or a listserv E-mail group to brainstorm and problem solve.

What are the minimum skills that an officer must have to do a good job in a community policing department? In addition to specific law enforcement skills, the officers must exhibit superior communication and interpersonal skills to thrive in this collaborative, problem-solving environment. Perhaps the most important attribute that the officer can bring to the job is a commitment to lifelong learning and growth. The problems in the community may not change as much as we think, but our ability to understand grows, and officers must be able to adapt to changing times and changing needs. Departments used to think of training as something that eventually stopped, but community policing requires expanding and updating skills and concepts throughout the officer's career.

Does emphasizing a "new breed" of officer mean that past and present officers are not suited for community policing? The danger in the rhetoric of reform is that it can imply that only new recruits, young, fresh, and untainted, are open-minded enough to embrace new ideas. Clearly, nothing could be further from the truth. All departments have burnouts of all ages, and all departments have energetic and inspired officers of all ages. The key is whether the officer understands the philosophy and its potential and is willing to work hard to make it succeed.

Do you need officer visibility with community policing? It is a different kind of community visibility, not the traditional officer in uniform being seen on the street or patrolling in the car. The goal is to have officers visible at community meetings and doing personal and business security checks, being at schools, and attending other functions. It is the actions that make officers visible, not their mere presence on the street as a deterrent to crime.

Should the department treat community policing officers differently from traditional officers? That is the quandary. On the one hand, community policing officers often enjoy more flexible schedules, weekends off, and other benefits that can inspire jealousy. Many departments require community policing officers to come to roll call before going to their beats, not as much for the information that they will receive by attending, but to enhance communication and interaction with their peers. Yet it is this separateness that makes the job category so controversial. Community policing officers can act as the department's onsite community builders and problem solvers. Their ownership in the area and knowledge of their beat makes them exceptionally valuable to the department and to the community. Yet the less they are set apart from their peers, the less opportunity there is for backlash to build.

Is street survival training for community policing officers inconsistent with community policing? Community policing officers need to know who the "good guys" and the "bad guys" are in the neighborhoods. On the one hand, they do not need to be defensive and suspicious of everyone on the street. On the other hand, when it comes to dealing with dangerous perpetrators, they need all of the help they can get, ranging from citizen help to a knowledge of techniques that will help them survive on the street.

How should the department deal with prejudiced officers? If officers with personal biases allow their personal feelings to influence their actions, their misbehavior must be uncovered and sanctioned, and they should be retrained to avoid any repetition. If the individuals can overcome their biases and behave appropriately on the job, they may be fit for continuing duty. However, there is concern that the stresses of the job could cause prejudice to interfere with their performance in the future, so they may require special supervision and vigilance. All of us harbor some misperceptions and preconceived notions, but the goal is to embrace tolerance and be sensitive to the need to learn all we can about the broad spectrum of people in our communities.

How do you teach acceptance of risk-taking and support for the freedom to fail? This is not an easy challenge in training, but the ultimate determinant is support within the department. The only way that people will feel free to innovate and try new ideas is when they see others try and fail without ridicule or sanction. Indeed the lesson for all training is that good intentions are no more than hot air if they do not translate into actions that model behavior for others.

Why does job satisfaction improve with community policing? Job satisfaction improves with community policing because of job enhancement and job enlargement, as noted above. What this means in practice is that officers are challenged to do more than respond to calls; they are asked to solve problems. If we think of factory workers on the line, their biggest frustration stems from not being able to see how their contributions fit into the final product. Community policing allows officers at all levels and in different assignments new opportunities for follow-through, so that they can see the positive impact that their efforts make in the community.

What is the appropriate role for the community in training? Experience shows that training opportunities where police and formal and informal community leaders work together to learn about leadership, community building, and problem solving can produce dramatic, long-term results. Yet that remains an uncommon model. Police departments must try harder to do what it takes to bring the community to the table for training. There are also promising new efforts, such as the Center for Community Leadership, founded by Carl S. Taylor of Michigan State University, that offer new opportunities for community members to gain the information and the skills needed to work with police as equal partners and promote community policing from the grass-roots community level.

SECTION VI
Management, Supervision, Program Assessment, Performance Evaluation, and Promotion

Inverting the Police Pyramid

The management structure of police agencies has traditionally reflected the hierarchical pyramid, with the chief at the apex issuing orders that ultimately carry down to the line-level officers, who serve as the pawns marching across the chessboard. This kind of top-down system is designed to promote obedience through a one-way information flow. Those at the top are presumed to have the wisdom to know what should be done, so they are invested with the power to issue the orders that are designed to turn their vision and goals into reality. Even down to the uniforms, with their insignia for rank, the system is designed to function on the military model of command and control.

**PARAMILITARY
MODEL**

CHIEF

**Police
Department**

LINE-LEVEL OFFICERS

Community policing essentially turns that model on its head, by proposing that the function of management is instead to provide leadership and support to line level, where the officers do the important work. As we have learned, the community policing model also re-defines the work, to focus on community building and problem solving. Community policing therefore reflects acknowledgment of the theory that modern management, at its simplest, is the art of getting the work done through others, with supervision as the system to ensure the work is done well.

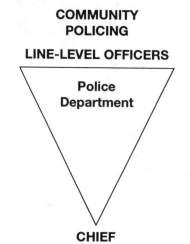

**COMMUNITY
POLICING**

LINE-LEVEL OFFICERS

Police
Department

CHIEF

Creating a Supportive Environment

The truth is, of course, that the paramilitary model functioned far differently in practice than it did in theory, because of the tremendous discretion that line-level officers have always had. The role of police officer offers the widest possible range of duties in society, since it is the one that permits the use of deadly force as part of the range of appropriate responses. Even though the traditional police management model treats officers as interchangeable pawns, the best have always used their individual power, within the scope of the job, to perform community building and problem solving. In many ways, community policing acknowledges, expands, and supports the unofficial and informal aspects of the job that officers have always done to make sure that the broad range of problems in the community were solved.

Community policing also proposes a management system built on trust and encouragement rather than fear and control. The old pyramid was based on the concept that people would goof off or go astray without constant supervision – it was built on addressing the problem of the worst employees.

Community policing instead builds its management model on supporting and maximizing the opportunities for the best employees to succeed. The tactics and techniques for fulfilling the community policing model of management and supervision include:

- **Facilitating** – This refers to the responsibility of police managers and supervisors to exercise their power to assist the line-level officers in their community-building and problem-solving activities. It can mean identifying and securing necessary resources – overtime pay, supplies, donations. It can mean cutting red tape, which often means modifying the policies, procedures, and practices that can get in the way. Or it can mean identifying contacts within other agencies, for example, the drug counselor willing to give priority to a candidate who needs help now. It can mean defusing the internal or external politics that can often pose the most serious threats to success.

- **Modeling** – This puts added responsibility on police managers and supervisors to model the behavior that they want officers to exhibit in the field. This means that if managers and supervisors want their officers to interact directly with citizens on community building and problem solving, they must do so themselves – management and supervision are no longer desk jobs. If they want their officers to assemble problem-solving teams to deal with specific issues, the way to model that behavior is to do the same thing to deal with internal obstacles and roadblocks. Clearly as well, how issues of internal diversity are handled serve as a model for how they should be handled in the community. While some will complain that it is "political correctness" and that jokes based on gender, race, ethnicity, religion, sexual preference, and other issues of diversity are an integral part of reducing tensions in police departments, it is time to recognize that encouraging civility, courtesy, and respect in the community requires modeling that behavior inside the agency. Again, the adage "do what I say, not what I do" will no longer be accepted in a community policing agency.

- **Coaching** – Not everyone can be as good at motivation as the late Green Bay Packers coach, Vince Lombardi. However, there are times when it makes sense to remind everyone of the vision that drives this new philosophy, since it is inspiring. The coach is also responsible for deciding on the immediate plays that make up the game plan that makes the vision ultimately achievable.

- **Mentoring** – In this role, police managers and supervisors can guide by sharing knowledge gleaned by experience, and also by passing along information and wisdom from a wide variety of sources. Canada's Chris Braiden says that he learned a lot about community policing during snowy days on traffic duty when he would watch the rabbits frolic and read about Ghandi or Martin Luther King, Jr. It would be nice to think that dog-eared copies of those books are still circulating within the department.

All four are offered as tactics and techniques to create a positive and supportive atmosphere within the agency, both for managers and supervisors themselves.

Support for Managers and Supervisors

Successful implementation of community policing as a department-wide change depends on strong leadership from the top. For the chief and top command to demonstrate their support to middle-management and first-line supervisors, they should:

- practice community policing internally by involving everyone in the department, especially middle managers and first-line supervisors, in the planning process as soon as possible;

- treat middle managers and first-line supervisors as a valuable source of information, ideas, and experience;

- provide clear and concise job descriptions for all assignments;

- avoid the temptation to dump problem employees into community-building or problem-solving assignments, or to use such assignments as punishment;

- demonstrate consistent, sustained support for middle managers and first-line supervisors who make well-intentioned mistakes; and

- shield middle managers and first-line supervisors from political interference.

Support for Line-Level Officers

Middle managers and first-line supervisors must in turn:

- treat officers as respected colleagues with good ideas and instincts;

- encourage autonomy and independence by avoiding the temptation to micromanage;

- foster creativity through brainstorming sessions;

- pitch in directly on occasion, to demonstrate that the supervisor is not asking anyone to do things that he or she would not do;

- create opportunities for formal and informal training and cross-fertilization with other departments;

- cut red tape – never add to it;

- identify resources and contacts within the community that the officers can access;

- carry the message to upper command about the resources that officers need to do the best job; and

- emphasize officers' triumphs to supervisors whenever possible, giving credit to the officers.

What Sergeants Want

In talking with sergeants from around the country who are trying to make community policing work, we have gathered a list of their concerns. Many feel that their voices are not always heard clearly in the planning process. They often feel that there is not sufficient appreciation for the difficulties inherent in the job, particularly when rules or procedures hinder more than help. The following is a wish list that they believe would help them succeed in their jobs:

- More authority and independence;

- Clearer role definition;

- More feedback, understanding, and backing from administration;

- More input into policy-making and decisionmaking;

- More training; more in-service schools;

- Relief from paperwork;

- More resources;

- More recognition for contribution and "less scapegoating"; and

- Insight into the "big picture" and reasons behind administrative decisions.

The Issue of Burnout

Police work has always had its own unique blend of stresses, but community policing adds to stress levels by promoting greater interaction with the community. The French existentialist Jean-Paul Sartre insisted that "hell is other people," and more than one police officer might be quick to agree.

Police managers and supervisors themselves may be at greater risk of burnout, and they have an added responsibility to deal with and prevent the problem in those they oversee. The opportunity to see results in the community can lure people into doing too much, which can sabotage their own health and the initiatives at hand. The following is offered for first-line supervisors, but it can be applied to managers and supervisors as well:

- Talk with officers about the need to maintain balance in their lives;

- Encourage officers to take their allotted time off;

- Be on the lookout for signs that community residents are manipulating the officers into doing things that they should be doing for themselves;

- Encourage officers not to neglect their families;

- Make sure that officers are not doing the work that other service agencies should be doing. Discuss strategies with both the officers and your supervisors on how to enlist the direct help of other service agencies who should do their share;

- Be alert to signs of burnout: fatigue, changes in personality, complaints from spouses, overuse of alcohol, frequent illness or accidents;

- Where appropriate, urge officers under stress to take advantage of counseling services the department may offer (or exhibit leadership in urging the department to provide them); and

- Remember to listen and offer help when the pressures become intense. Officers cannot read minds; they should be told to turn to their supervisors for help.

Official and Unofficial Rewards

The most successful community policing officers tend to be self-starters who derive satisfaction from knowing that they are doing their best to make a difference. That does not mean, however, that they do not want and need a pat on the back for a job well done. Probably the most important rewards the officer receives are the intangibles like "attaboys" from peers and compliments from residents of the community. The days of "Your reward is your paycheck" are long gone (but you cannot expect quality work for substandard pay).

First-line supervisors can reward excellence by:

- praising officers, privately and in front of their peers;

- nominating officers for departmental awards. (If community building and community-based problem solving do not qualify under the current awards program, efforts should be made to change the rules to do so.);

- demonstrating trust and support by flexibility (For example, community-based officers who are doing a good job should be allowed to work the flexible schedules they recommend, without needing to provide excessive justification and documentation.).

Program Assessment

Before building a performance evaluation for any specific job, the department must decide how to define success. Moving from quantitative to qualitative assessments of activities and programs means focusing on problems solved. However, as we noted in previous sections, community policing redefines success to include harm reduction – such as fewer people affected; a problem that is still there but less visible; or fewer new problems erupting.

Before a department can determine whether an individual is successful in his or her job, the department needs to decide on parameters for the success or failure of any initiative. To encourage risk-taking, even apparent failures must be considered as worthwhile expenditures of time and resources, if it was a well-intentioned and carefully planned effort, and if the reasons for failure are documented and shared.

Performance Evaluations

Why do departments evaluate individual employees? Under the old pyramid, the focus was often on documenting failure to justify dismissal without triggering a lawsuit. While there are times that that may be necessary, if that is all that your performance evaluation system accomplishes, it does not do enough to support the changes required by community policing.

The following are offered as useful goals in crafting individual performance evaluations, regardless of rank:

- Document an individual officer's performance;
- Provide some basis for comparing an officer's performance to the job description/task inventory;
- Serve as a foundation for future goals for the individual evaluated;
- Identify, document, analyze, and disseminate information about effective strategies and tactics that the individual employed, so that others can benefit;
- Do the same for efforts that failed, to warn others of potential pitfalls;
- Contribute data to assessments of the impact and effectiveness of the changes made to implement community policing;
- Assist in assessing individual and collective training needs;
- Provide documentation useful to public policymakers, civic officials, and funders/donors;
- Assist the individual in establishing goal-directed activities toward specific problems;

- Assist the individual in assessing his or her progress in making a positive difference in the community, through leadership, community building and problem solving, and to assess progress in specific projects; and

- Provide a foundation for evaluation of individuals for promotion.

Building an Evaluation

To assess individual performance requires knowing what the job is supposed to involve, and that benefits from developing a job description that is based on an accurate task inventory/job analysis. Identifying the tasks; determining their relative contribution to the goals of leadership, community building, and problem solving; and collapsing them into the elements of a job description can be accomplished in different ways. Some attempt to identify tasks by observing individuals on the job, noting time spent in different functions. Many simply discuss with the people doing the work how they spend their time in practice and as compared to the ideal. Remember that these tools should express elements of the work, not personality or character traits.

The challenge, however, is to move beyond quantifying activity toward identifying ways to tell whether the activities result in good-faith efforts to solve problems. It matters less whether officers spend 20 percent of their time in meetings than whether the time spent succeeds in community building or problem solving, and how that translates into positive change in the community.

One of the more promising evaluation strategies places the burden for "building the case" on the officer. The supervisor can challenge the officer to document his or her activity in community building and problem solving, accompanied by an analysis of the success or failure of those efforts. The goal is to tie activity to outcome.

It would be up to the officer to provide "proof," which could range from a video showing that a problem corner looks better to statements from community residents that the problem with prostitution on weekends has been reduced to reductions in target crime rates. From there, the discussion would proceed to setting appropriate goals for the next time period. The goal is to move from a system that focuses on detecting mistakes and problems to one that supports and enhances opportunities for success.

Support for Team Building

Community policing often adopts a team approach to problems. Strategies can include assigning patrol officers to specific problem-solving teams that are then assigned to a neighborhood. They can meet and confer by other means (including E-mail) on a regular basis. In this approach, it is ownership of the geographic area that determines team membership, and the team is challenged to recruit members of the community to become partners in problem solving. Clearly, reaching that goal may require investing time first in community building.

Another strategy is to assemble teams based on specific problems. There is growing awareness of (and often new legislation aimed at) stalking, for example, yet it may not surface as a priority within problem-solving teams organized by turf, so leadership from top command may be needed to focus attention on the problem. In this case, the department might assemble a special team that includes police and representatives from various groups within the community to engage in problem solving aimed at developing a variety of strategies to deal with the problem. Those strategies might well include involving the geographically based teams – to gather information from the community, to identify specific victims and perpetrators, and to brainstorm on solving the problems. The individual's performance evaluation may well become wedded to the overall performance of various teams.

The following shows the kind of performance evaluation that could be considered to document and assess individual and team efforts.

Sample Performance Evaluation Analysis Report

Hot Spot/Affordable Housing

Three months ago, community residents in a low-income neighborhood expressed concern about a growing number of problems with drug dealing and prostitution in the neighborhood. Officers X and Y met with area leaders twice to host a series of meetings to gain information and focus on problem solving. However, participation was lower than expected. The officers recruited the principal at the local elementary school and an area minister, and both agreed to host a Saturday afternoon Puppet Show where flyers about the next meeting were handed out. At the next meeting, attendance was up and two community leaders agreed to develop a plan to establish citizen patrols to assist law enforcement in confronting the customers of the drug dealers and prostitutes. The officers agreed to talk with area businesses about donating to a fund for jackets, radios, and bullhorns for the group.

Officer X worked with Sergeant A to identify landlords at problem sites, many of whom do not live in the neighborhood. They met with the landlord who was identified as the biggest problem, and they brought letters from residents about their concerns. The landlord has agreed to evict problem tenants (who were behind on their rent anyhow), and Officers X and Y have agreed to attend rental showings, whenever possible, to send a message that drug dealers are not welcome.

(continued from previous page)

> Officer Y had a meeting with code officials, on putting together a community-based team to work together on upgrading housing stocks without triggering gentrification that can put affordable housing out of the reach of low-income residents. The officers were able to make improvements in six homes, and they were able to assist in resolving three landlord/tenant disputes. One officer is working on finding a location for a community meeting on the rights and responsibilities of landlords and tenants. The officer has also found a donor who will supply deadbolt locks to those tenants who need them.

The challenge with narratives is that it is difficult to extract the kinds of statistical data that policymakers and politicians often demand and that the media find so attractive. "Crime is up (or down) 10% this year" is an easier nugget to verify and transmit than "officers have invested greater effort in community building and solving a wide variety of problems in the community." The reality is, of course, that funding decisions are often made on the basis of statistics, so the challenge becomes inventing ways to make the numbers reflect real results in the community.

Promotion

Performance evaluations typically function as part of the information used to determine promotions. With the transition to community policing, however, the goal also requires revisiting the promotional process to see if it can be made to do a better job of identifying, certifying, and promoting individuals who express leadership for community building and problem solving.

Identifying appropriate criteria for all personnel requires working backward from the vision of the ideal candidate to the skills and tasks implicit in the job. Remember also that promotional criteria must be bias-free. Women, for example, have been disadvantaged by the listing qualities typically associated with males: strong, forceful, determined. Best to leave the adjectives out and focus on what individuals should do to perform well in the role.

In addition to written promotional exams that allow candidates to demonstrate knowledge, oral examinations should be held in front of a panel that includes the community. Those exams should focus on assessing the candidate's ability to put knowledge into practice and on the candidate's judgment. (A variation on oral exams is the "in-basket" test that asks for written responses to scenarios that mirror the realities of the job.) In addition to open-ended questions, the panel should also be prepared with real-life scenarios that require leadership in applying the principles of community policing internally and externally:

- *Sergeant as Facilitator* **Scenario** - Officers who have been working with residents of a public housing development on the issue of preventing domestic violence approach you, the sergeant, with a list of ideas generated at their last meeting. The initial plan is to host a series of coffees in the morning once a week to talk about the issue and open up dialogue about how more can be done. They need speakers, and they want to hand out brochures on the problem. One idea is to have copies of the forms to file personal protection orders available there, but they are not sure whether that is legal. How do you help them succeed?

- *Sergeant as Problem Solver* **Scenario** - A lieutenant tells you that he and others have heard a specific officer under your command making jokes that are racist and sexist, and that there have been times when these have been disruptive. What is your strategy to deal with the problem?

The inclusion of members of the community on the panel contributes to community building, by demonstrating a willingness to open up the process. After all, if the community is the ultimate consumer of police services, it makes sense to include them in decisions that will shape the culture of the department over time.

Questions and Answers

The theme of leadership at all levels seems to run through all of the discussions about implementing community policing. How will we know when we have it? When it is as likely that a good idea comes from the bottom as from the top. When everyone in the department, regardless of rank and including non-sworn and civilian personnel, expresses the philosophy and Ten Principles automatically. When community building and problem solving are used to deal with problems within the department and in the community. When those who exhibit leadership in this regard are supported, rewarded, and promoted.

What is the biggest change for management with implementation of community policing? The biggest change is that the manager must shift from controller to facilitator, which literally turns the organization upside down. It recognizes that the real work of the department is done at line level, and that the role of management should be to provide vision, direction, structure, planning, and resources - and also to get out of the way.

How can we develop qualitative performance evaluations that focus on outcomes when we are constantly being asked for statistical data to justify that these changes are worth it? Performance evaluations must serve many purposes, and satisfying policymakers, politicians, community leaders, and public, corporate, and foundation funders who depend on statistical data to make decisions is a valid goal. As we grow more sophisticated about the many faces of success that community policing can produce, there may be opportunities to capture new sources of data. Harm reduction strategies often allow "counting" and quantifying improvements that might have previously been overlooked.

Is it realistic to expect any police official to provide public support for a project that fails? There appears to be a growing thirst among citizens for leaders who express candor and honesty. This does not mean that bungles or disasters can or should be explained away. But a well-designed and well-planned effort that simply does not work or which included well-intentioned mistakes can be justified as worth trying – far better than not trying. The challenge is to articulate the reasons that risk-taking must be part of community policing, which is that the system must change from one that focused primarily on CYA (cover-your-anatomy) to one that encourages people inside and outside the department to stick out their individual and collective necks for initiatives that deserve a chance at making the community a better and safer place.

How can managers and supervisors encourage teamwork? First of all, they can do so by modeling it in their relationships with each other. Second, they can build rewards for exhibiting teamwork into performance evaluations, promotional criteria, and honors. Third, they can facilitate teamwork by changing the policies, practices, and procedures that have made doing so more difficult. Fourth, they can bring resources to bear (such as by accessing overtime pay to allow cross-shift collaboration). Fifth, they can coach and mentor officers along the way.

Are community policing proponents rising within the ranks? Evidence that those who made a commitment to community policing are being rewarded for their leadership is evidenced in the second wave of leadership that is moving up. The first wave of pioneers such as Lee Brown of New York City and Drew Diamond of Tulsa has moved up and out. (Brown became drug czar before returning to academe and then becoming Mayor of Houston, and Diamond works with the Police Executive Research Forum, including a rotation as PERF's director of the Community Policing Consortium in Washington, DC). The second wave is moving up into the chief's office, and the third wave is following close behind.

SECTION VII
The Future of Community Policing

Applying the Principles

The change embodied in the philosophic shift to community policing is profound. Making the transition requires more than stationing a few officers in high-crime beats, and it goes beyond working smarter by using problem-solving techniques and crime analysis.

Community policing fundamentally changes the nature of the relationship between people and their police by recognizing that collaborating as partners enhances decisionmaking at every level. The quality of the decisions made and their support in the community are enhanced when the police and the community work together as equals, regardless of whether the problem is an imminent danger posed by a serial rapist, the chronic disorder of low-level drug dealing, or a quality-of-life concern such as panhandling on the street.

At the chief's level, collaboration often means regular brainstorming sessions with a leadership council comprised of community leaders, business professionals, educators, academics, and leaders of the faith community. At the neighborhood level, the partnership typically takes the form of regular meetings between officers and community residents, to build community and solve problems. Those who have witnessed firsthand the power and quality of decisionmaking that occurs when people of different views, skills, and experience collaborate as partners understand how radically community policing alters the status quo.

The question therefore becomes how the lessons learned from community policing can be applied to other institutions perceived as losing touch with the community. Without overstating the case, declining voter turnout is a symptom of a larger malaise – a growing sense that average citizens have little to gain from the system and little opportunity to make public institutions work for them. The rise of the militia movement reflects a loss of faith in state

and federal government by many blue-collar workers and rural residents who
see their way of life threatened by the global economy. Even victim groups
feel frustrated that they have not yet passed the federal victims' rights amend-
ment that grants them rights that many people assume victims already have,
such as the right to speak at sentencing and the right to be notified of
changes in the offender's status. There is a growing sense that we have not
kept pace in developing mechanisms that allow the voices of average citizens
to be heard.

The principles embodied in community policing therefore point the way
toward a total community approach, where partnership with the community
becomes the cornerstone for populist reform. (See the chart below.) Trust,
accountability, problem solving, partnership, equity, service, change, vision,
empowerment, and leadership are principles that can serve as the foundation
for broad-ranging public reform.

The police themselves have argued that they were forced to implement
community policing by default more than by choice. As the only public service agency open and available 24 hours a day, seven days a week, the police
could not avoid the demands of the community to improve public safety, particularly when crack cocaine began to exploit the shortcomings of the existing system. Yet the police arguably found themselves assuming roles in the
community that could better be handled by others, and there are promising
efforts to use the community policing model for systemic reform.

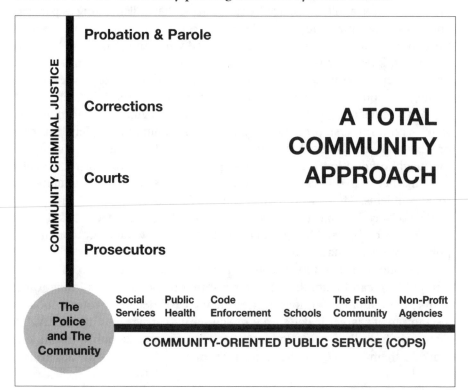

A Total Community Approach

We do not have a criminal justice or public service "system," but a con-glomeration of separate fiefdoms, each with its own culture, turf battles, and agenda. Much of the public's frustration stems from discovering that they have little power to engage the various elements of the system on their behalf or to make it perform as advertised.

Problems run the gamut from minor glitches to outright horror stories – the failure to notify victims and witnesses when court dates change; the land-lord who scoffs at code enforcement rules; the sentence of community ser-vice that never happens because no one is checking; and the buck-passing as agency after agency announces, "It's not our job."

Sometimes the frustrations do little more than raise our blood pressure. But other failures cannot be easily dismissed. One mother whose daughter was murdered cannot find out why the perpetrator's sentence has been changed. A Michigan mother, whose daughter was raped and strangled in New Orleans, no longer has her phone calls returned by the detective on the case. Yet another mother of a murdered daughter receives conflicting reports about whether there is sufficient DNA evidence for testing against future sus-pects. All feel that they are being sent a message by the professionals that they should leave the case to the experts, even though doing so has yet to bring satisfaction. If people with such serious problems feel ignored and neglected, imagine the treatment that people with relatively minor concerns must endure.

It does not really matter whether the abuses are systemic or whether they are just isolated incidents. The issue is how we can reinvent a public sector that does a better job of delivering on its promises with courtesy and respect. And in an era when taxpayers are constantly regaled with political rhetoric about how they are paying too much for inadequate services, a failure to pro-vide people a much-needed voice in how those services will be delivered threatens the very future of the public sector. Again and again, we hear the cry that privatization is the answer to enhanced accountability, and the best hedge against that is a system that meets the needs of those it is supposed to serve.

A Community Criminal Justice System

What would a community criminal justice system look like? We have seen glimmers in the efforts of Montgomery County, Maryland, to decentralize and personalize the prosecutor's office. Instead of dividing up the work by type of crime, the workload depends on geography, where the prosecutor works with police in the community on the full roster of cases in the area. Miami's drug courts and New York City's neighborhood courts show how the judicial branch could move closer to the community.

Just as with community policing, forging closer ties between police, prosecutors, courts, and community serves as a reminder that quality-of-life issues cannot be ignored. The community expects the system to work in the most serious cases of rape, murder, robbery, and assault, but they also want solutions to problems such as the prostitutes on the corner, and the kids on the street late at night. Involving prosecutors and courts at the grass-roots level helps them to grasp the importance of working with the community on what might otherwise seem to be insignificant quality-of-life concerns.

Restorative Justice

Moving toward a community approach means exploring opportunities afforded by restorative justice. Restorative (as opposed to retributive) justice is based on the premise that those who harm the community should be made to undo at least part of the damage they cause.

A youngster arrested for graffiti could be sentenced to spend the next six months painting over graffiti each weekend. A resident repeatedly cited for his or her barking dog might be required to put in 100 hours at the local animal shelter. Restorative justice recognizes that increasing fines or threatening jail time do little to drive home an understanding of how bad behavior corrodes community life. The creative sentencing inherent in restorative justice provides a way to use the system to reinforce the message that even so-called petty offenses take a toll on everyone's quality of life.

Research confirms that even those people who advocate tougher sentencing support efforts to ensure greater equity. What most people want is a system that reliably keeps the most violent offenders off the street, at least until there is some realistic hope that they will not harm us again. Of concern is that lengthening sentences for nonviolent offenses underlies the problem of decaying schools versus shiny new prisons.

Jail and prison cells are scarce and expensive commodities that should be used to greatest effect, particularly when it comes to "sending a message about drugs." Public outrage about drugs has resulted in the passage of new mandatory minimum sentences for a broad range of federal and state drug offenses. Contrary to popular opinion, even marijuana prosecutions consume enormous resources. FBI data show that 535,000 people were arrested for possession, sale, or manufacture of marijuana, hashish, or hashish oil in 1992, with life sentences imposed in six cases. But what the politicians are less eager to explain to taxpayers is that there are only a limited number of ways to carry out those new mandates:

- Build more cells to house these nonviolent offenders for longer terms;

- Jam more prisoners into existing facilities, which inevitably increases the violence that often makes those who have served time more dangerous than they were before their imprisonment;

- Reduce expenses by cutting staff, which puts the remaining guards at even greater risk; and/or

- Release offenders sentenced under less stringent guidelines earlier.

The only other option is privatization. Yet it is not at all clear whether privatizing jails and prisons actually saves money, since they must provide the same level of service for less and yet pay profits to owners and stockholders. In many cases, this means substituting non-unionized labor; providing less training; and cutting the amounts spent for prisoners' food, clothing, and medical care. The shocking video footage of private correctional officers in Texas assaulting contract prisoners from others states also raises serious questions about public accountability.

There was justifiable outrage when a violent felon (and repeat offender) in Florida who held two youngsters hostage at gunpoint was found to have served roughly one year of a 12-year sentence, because of prison overcrowding. While unpopular with many voters, the solution may require reducing the mandatory minimum sentence for the woman who carries a suitcase full of cocaine for a fee of $200, so that keeping her behind bars, as we support her children, does not force the early release of the serial rapist or murderer sentenced under less stringent guidelines.

Community Efforts Seek to Keep Serial Killer Behind Bars

An example of community criminal justice collaboration is the committee that formed to deal with the threatened release of serial killer Donald Gene Miller, who murdered four women in the Lansing area in the mid-1970s. Miller was apprehended shortly after raping a young girl and stabbing her brother in a neighboring county. Complications in building a case for the murders resulted in a plea bargain that will result in his release – not parole but release – in February 1999.

Periodically over the years, victims, police, and prosecutors involved with the case would voice concern. Yet there was no mechanism for them to work together. Then, in 1996, a small group concerned about Miller's release began to meet informally every couple months or so at a local resident's home. Jay Kohl, the former chief of Meridian Township, a suburb of Lansing, later offered his department's facilities for more formal bi-monthly meetings.

The group named itself C-CAP, the Committee for Community Awareness and Protection. The roster initially consisted of representatives from the police agencies that had investigated the case; area prosecutors; a concerned psychiatrist; the head of the Michigan Victim Alliance (two board members still live within one mile of the

(continued from previous page)

Miller family); and the former prosecutor (now judge) who struck the plea bargain. The membership has grown to include almost 30 members, including the survivors of Miller's attack and family members of other victims.

C-CAP used the meetings to share news and information. A legislative subcommittee, organized by C-CAP chair Frank Ochberg, the former director of the Michigan Department of Mental Health, began work in anticipation of the Supreme Court decision on civil commitment of serial sexual offenders. At one meeting, a corrections officer told how Miller had lost "good time," as a result of administrative sanctions imposed when a garrote was found in his cell. At another session, an investigator proposed pursuing the possibility that Miller might have killed others, in the hope that he could be prosecuted for these new crimes. Others explored the possibility of indicting Miller on federal civil rights charges, since he killed women, who are a protected class.

Eaton County prosecutor Jeff Sauter, who had put Miller away for the attack on the youngsters in his jurisdiction, remembers leaving one C-CAP meeting feeling especially uneasy. "Something kept nagging at me," he said. Then Sauter flashed on the possibility of prosecuting Miller criminally for the weapon that was found in his cell. Michigan law allows stacking criminal penalties on top of the administrative sanctions that had already been imposed.

Sauter contacted fellow C-CAP member Stuart Dunnings, the current Ingham County prosecutor, and together they approached the Chippewa County prosecutor, who has jurisdiction in the matter, and Miller is now facing trial on the weapons charges. Sauter credits the collaboration with giving him the idea. "If it hadn't been for the ideas brought up at a C-CAP meeting, I would have never put it all together," he said.

No one knows yet whether any of these efforts will ultimately prove successful in keeping Miller incarcerated. So the legislative committee continues to organize testimony to shape a civil commitment statute for Michigan that would be narrowly crafted, but which would not let Miller escape its net. The committee also continues to develop strategies to warn the community without inciting panic should Miller be released. In addition, C-CAP members decided to share what they have learned, by hosting a major training conference on the serial/sexual predator, designated as the first in the Robert Trojanowicz series, in honor of his commitment to community collaboration.

Providing the community a seat at the table when tough choices about such trade-offs are made not only allows them to have input, but it educates citizens about the complexity of the issues and the difficulty in making wise choices. They can then serve as the system's ombudsmen to the community, helping to explain why there are few if any easy answers to these complex decisions. People within the system often complain that citizens do not understand their problems. Giving average people and paid professionals the chance to work together helps all sides understand each other.

Community-Oriented Public Service

The logic of extending the Ten Principles of community policing to the delivery of other public services is underscored by the recent election of Lee Brown as mayor of Houston. Brown, who holds a Ph.D. in criminal justice, first had the opportunity to implement his ideas about community policing as chief in Atlanta. Then he became chief in Houston, followed by a term as police commissioner of New York City under Mayor David Dinkins. Brown served as federal drug czar, before returning to academe, and he has now emerged as mayor of the city where he was once chief.

Without reading too much into a single example, Brown's election can be viewed not only as a vindication of the past history of community policing in Houston, but as a symbol of how the same principles that informed police reform can offer a model for revitalizing the delivery of all city services. After Brown left Houston for New York, the city was run by Mayor Kathy Whitmire and Police Chief Elizabeth (Betsy) Watson, a rare case where two women held the two top posts. Fears of a "crime wave" subsequently swept both women out of office in 1991, fueled by the argument that a back-to-basics, rapid response, crime-specific police approach was the answer. This apparent rejection of community policing by the electorate in Houston added fuel to critics' contentions that community policing offers no enduring success stories.

Yet, as we approach the turn of the twenty-first century, there is renewed recognition that the vision and values reflected in the Ten Principles provide a better way of delivering services to the community. Tough as they are to institute – and institutionalize – these principles provide the best model yet to deliver on promises of effectiveness and accountability.

These new ideas began to surface in the early 1990s. James Pinkerton, a White House aide in the Bush administration, talked about a "new paradigm," which has been echoed by Vice President Al Gore's commitment to "reinventing government." David Osborne and Ted Gaebler, in their 1992 book titled *Reinventing Government: How the Entrepreneurial Spirit Is Transforming the Public Sector,* proposed five Cs as the foundation:

- **Core** (clarify purposes);
- **Consequences** (create incentives for employee performance);

- **Customer** (structure feedback from those who receive the services);

- **Control** (empower people to do what is needed); and

- **Culture** (replace old habits with new commitments).

In the public sector, these changes can mean that departments get to keep unspent funds at the end of the year, to use on special projects, thereby encouraging managers both to trim costs and to experiment. It is not yet possible to point to any one city as a shining example of a total community approach, but efforts continue to grow nationwide.

On the other hand, many of the questions raised about community policing surface in regard to these broad-based government reforms. Is community-oriented public service a substantive reform or a clever new buzzword? How can communities evaluate these new efforts in terms that persuade politicians to sign on? (It is easier to quantify activity than to capture improvements in quality of life and problems solved.)

Controversial as well is that these reforms are built on a model of trust rather than one of control. Do we really trust civil servants well enough to give them new freedoms to innovate? Will politicians tolerate the inevitable failures to continue promoting innovation and risk-taking?

It may also prove difficult to generate broad-based support for a total community approach. Community policing involves life-and-death issues of crime and violence, so people care when statistics confirm a dramatic downturn in violent crime, attributable at least in part to community policing reform. It is harder to get media attention and thereby community support for streamlining the bureaucracy in other departments.

Community Leadership

A total community approach asks even more of the jurisdiction's residents. For such broad-based reform to work, the community needs education and training on how to be full and equal partners in the public process. Without leadership training for the community, residents risk being manipulated, ignored, or kept from the table when the going gets rough.

As Trojanowicz used to say, the only drawback in targeting community engagement as the goal is that we should be talking marriage instead, where the partners make a commitment to each other to work through the problems, no matter what it takes. The goal is to reach the point where the community can deal with an ever-greater share of its problems without requiring the intervention or assistance of government, with all its obvious and hidden costs.

Community Policing in Cyberspace

The advent of mass transportation and mass communication during this past century have forever changed society in ways we may not yet fully comprehend, changing the police process as well. Yet there is a sense that the accelerating pace of change, as we approach the beginning of the twenty-first century, will challenge our wildest imagination.

On one hand are the optimists who envision a technological nirvana free of poverty, drudgery, inhumanity, and evil. Others see us dividing further into informational, educational, and economic haves and have-nots, with all the potential for mistrust and savagery between countries, communities, and individuals that such divisions imply.

New Categories of Online Crime

No one can say with certainty which future will prevail, but what we can safely predict is that the police will face new opportunities and new pitfalls. About the latter, the police already find themselves being asked to do more to protect us in the new informational environment of the Internet and the World Wide Web.

All of the old financial scams – and some new ones – are finding vulnerable victims on the Internet. Add to that the new crime of cyberstalking, where an unknown someone who may live near or far can target a person for anonymous harassment. Most disturbing perhaps are opportunities for pedophiles to target young prey in Internet chat rooms. As one so-called cyberlawyer explains, parents do not yet recognize that the Internet is not Disneyland, and that even there, parents would not let their children wander unsupervised and encourage them to talk to strangers.

It can be difficult for police to develop workable strategies to deal with these new threats, particularly if the department's leadership resists joining the computer age. The police have not yet moved to address white-collar crime as vigorously as they should, and the new information society poses even greater challenges.

Police Department Web Sites

On the positive side, however, many departments have begun to build a community for themselves on the Internet. Each day, search engines verify that more police agencies are going online, launching their own Web sites.

Some are done thoughtfully, as part of a citywide effort. Others are clearly the work of a single passionate Web afficionado. The offerings vary wildly, in size, focus, scope, and interactivity, with some big-city sites clearly missing the mark, while other small-town departments have produced cutting-edge sites.

A number of police Web sites offer straightforward information about the department and its services. The Austin Police Department's Web site (http://www.ci.austin.tx.us/police) is one of the many well-planned and well executed police sites. The department uses the site to provide visitors with basic information, and it also serves as a tool for recruitment and as an online memorial to officers killed in the line of duty.

The Burlington (MA) Police Department's Web site (http://www.bpd.org) makes good use of this new technology by offering the E-mail addresses and photos of the staff, as well as a virtual tour of the police department. Unique as well is that the site offers cartoons on safety, created especially for the department by nationally known cartoonists.

A unique use of the Internet's interactivity can be found on the Nashville (TN) Police Department site (http://www.nashville.org/police_dept.html), which offers Danger High, a multimedia game on violence reduction for schools, as well as a play-by-play of a car chase. The Easton (MA) site (http://www.eastonpd.com) surprises by including thousands of special links for kids (even bedtime stories).

Another good idea comes from the San Gabriel (CA) (http://www.sgpd.com), which offers its own "Most Wanted" list. Truly ambitious is the Beaufort (SC) Police Department's site (http://bftpolice.com), with its daily update of calls for service and information on its domestic violence initiative. Long Beach (CA) also has a beautifully designed site (http://www.ci.long-beach.ca.us/lbpd/index.htm), which billboards news of interest.

Chicago (http://www.ci.chi.il.us) is making its site part of Chicago's Alternative Policing Strategy (CAPS), by offering visitors the chance to provide drug tips online. Visitors can also receive information on how to track individuals who have been convicted. Boston (http://www.ci.boston.ma.us/bpdtemp/index.htm) includes a case history of an older case, as well as an attractive page on the academy.

As this suggests, each site has its own character and appeal. Among the many cautions:

- **Respect Your Visitors and Honor the Technology** – Producing Web sites that work well is not easy. First of all, many people surf the Internet with the graphics turned off, or their vision is impaired, so you should make full use of the ALT tags to tell visitors what the graphics contain. Many people also have slow modems and older browsers – you will lose them, if your pages take too long to load. (Each page should contain no more than 40k total of text and graphics.) Also make sure to use the Web-safe palette, to ensure your colors appear the same on all browsers (http://www.lynda.com). Important as well is to think through your navigation strategy. (And if all of this seems like geeky gobbledygook, assign someone else the task of developing your Web site.)

- **Avoid Music and Other Jarring Bells and Whistles** – Many people surf the Internet at work, so you do them no favor when music and sound effects begin blaring from the speakers. (And because it can take many minutes for the music to load, unsuspecting visitors can find themselves jolted when the music kicks in.)

- **Update Constantly** – Broken links and outdated references are not the only reason to keep updating your site. Adding fresh materials is a great way to keep people coming back, which allows you to teach them more about the department and about what they can do to protect themselves. Things to consider including over time:

  - Neighborhood Watch listings;

  - Rosters of community meetings;

  - How to reach others – animal control, code enforcement, sanitation, prosecutors, courts, corrections;

  - Lost and found;

  - Surveys and message boards;

  - Education about the new forms of computer crime;

  - Forms and reports; and

  - Recruit volunteers from the community for specific kinds of help and allow them to sign up online.

The Michigan Victim Alliance received a grant from the U.S. Department of Justice's Office for Victims of Crime to develop the Michigan Crime Victims Web site (http://www.MIvictims.org), and it contains ideas that police departments should consider adopting. One major feature is that the site offers all of the forms that can be required to secure personal protection orders (domestic relationship and stalking), along with full instructions. The site also offers E-mail pen-pal support for victims, and periodic live chat opportunities (such as when Marc Klaas, the father of Polly Klaas – who was abducted and murdered – came to town).

The Healing & Recovery section provides messages of hope. And new sites should consider including links such as the one from the Center for Missing and Exploited Children that rotates photographs of a dozen children whose families hope that someone will recognize them. The goal is not to develop a cookie-cutter approach, but to continue building the site so that it can meet growing needs. It would be great if there were eventually a single registry for all of the police and criminal justice sites springing up around the country.

Web sites can be an important new tool in the department's community policing strategy. For one thing, involving the community in the development of the site makes excellent sense. When designed effectively, Web sites can reduce the number of telephone calls for basic information, thereby freeing personnel time. It can also generate information for the department on problems in the community.

Moreover, an Internet outreach addresses the common complaint that community policing primarily benefits the poor. A community policing Web site allows the department to build ties with those who are affluent enough to have their own computers. At the same time, building a department Web site now will help others, as they gain access. Microsoft's Bill Gates has pledged $200 million toward funding the installation of computers in public libraries, and the police could spearhead efforts to harness these new Internet outlets in addressing crime and disorder in the community.

Online Education and Problem Solving

Just a few years ago, entering the words "community policing" into a search engine generated no more than a handful of hotlinks. Now, the same request on Infoseek generates 2.8 million references – a vivid example of the growth in community policing and on the Internet. The World Wide Web has become an essential educational tool, allowing police officers to access information about cutting-edge applications of the community policing philosophy.

The Internet will soon provide police officers new opportunities to collaborate online, through listservs, chat rooms, and message boards to serve a variety of needs. The technology offers a chance for quick answers to questions ranging from where to find reliable radio repair to how to organize a citizen patrol. A chiefs' listserv could allow top command to share ideas on common concerns, ranging from budget problems to politics. Officers could do the same to provide each other peer support on issues of burnout, trauma, and stress.

A listserv including both the police and the community from all over the world could brainstorm together on important issues. What do people want from their police? How can we build coalitions that maintain their motivation? Are there any new strategies to reduce the potential for violence in schools? An investigator who hit a snag could ask for fresh ideas. The topics are limitless, and the opportunities for meaningful interaction are only beginning to emerge.

Our Inter-Connected World

Bob Trojanowicz died unexpectedly in 1994 at the age of 52, on the brink of community policing's full acceptance as the way that all police agencies should deliver service to the community. Bob recognized that community policing – and even a total community approach – cannot solve all of our problems with crime and disorder. Public safety ultimately rests on providing equal educational and economic opportunities. Even the wondrous technology of the Internet is only a tool. It can help us communicate with each other, but the real advances require a change of heart, so that we can build a society based on tolerance and mutual respect.

As the Internet shrinks our world even further, and the global economy reminds us how interdependent we truly are, Trojanowicz' words about community ring even more true today: "Until we are all safe, no one is safe."

APPENDIX A
The Ten Principles of Community Policing
(Earlier Version)

These Ten Principles should inform all policies, procedures, and practices associated with community policing. Many groups use them as a guide when writing their plans, referring to specific principles as justification for or explanation of certain decisions or actions.

1. **Philosophy and Organizational Strategy** – Community policing is both a philosophy (a way of thinking) and an organizational strategy (a way to carry out the philosophy) that allows the police and the community to work closely together in new ways to solve the problems of crime, illicit drugs, fear of crime, physical and social disorder (from graffiti to addiction), neighborhood decay, and the overall quality of life in the community. The philosophy rests on the belief that people deserve input into the police process, in exchange for their participation and support. It also rests on the belief that solutions to today's community problems demand freeing both community residents and the police to explore creative, new ways to address neighborhood concerns beyond a narrow focus on individual crime incidents.

2. **Commitment to Community Empowerment** – Community policing's organizational strategy first demands that everyone in the police department, including civilian, sworn, and non-sworn personnel, must investigate ways to translate the philosophy of power-sharing into practice. This demands making a subtle but sophisticated shift so that everyone in the department understands the need to focus on solving community problems in creative, new ways that can include challenging and enlightening people in the process of policing themselves. Community policing implies a shift within the department that grants greater autonomy (free-

109

dom to make decisions) to line officers, which also implies enhanced respect for their judgment as police professionals. Within the community, citizens must share in the rights and responsibilities implicit in identifying, prioritizing, and solving problems, as full-fledged partners with the police.

3. **Decentralized and Personalized Policing** – To implement true community policing, police departments must also create and develop a new breed of line officer who acts as a direct link between the police and the people in the community. As the department's community outreach specialists, community policing officers must be freed from the isolation of the patrol car and the demands of the police radio so that they can maintain daily, direct, face-to-face contact with the people they serve in a clearly defined beat area. Ultimately, all officers should practice the community policing approach.

4. **Immediate and Long-Term Proactive Problem Solving** – The community policing officer's broad role demands continuous, sustained contact with the law-abiding people in the community, so that together they can explore creative new solutions to local concerns, with private citizens serving as supporters and as volunteers. As law enforcement officers, community policing officers respond to calls for service and make arrests, but they also go beyond this narrow focus to develop and monitor broad-based, long-term initiatives that can involve all elements of the community in efforts to improve the overall quality of life. As the community's ombudsman, the community policing officer also acts as a link to other public and private agencies that can help in a given situation.

5. **Ethics, Legality, Responsibility, and Trust** – Community policing implies a new contract between the police and the citizens they serve, one that offers hope of overcoming widespread apathy while restraining any impulse of vigilantism. This new relationship, based on mutual trust and respect, also suggests that the police can serve as a catalyst, challenging people to accept their share of the responsibility for the overall quality of life in the community. Community policing means that citizens will be asked to handle more of their minor concerns themselves, but, in exchange, this will free police to work with people on developing immediate as well as long-term solutions for community concerns in ways that encourage mutual accountability and respect.

6. **Expanding the Police Mandate** – Community policing adds a vital, proactive element to the traditional reactive role of the police, resulting in full-spectrum police service. As the only agency of social control open 24 hours a day, seven days a week, the police must maintain the ability to respond immediately to crises and crime incidents, but community polic-

ing broadens the police role so that they can make a greater impact on making changes today that hold the promise of making communities safer and more attractive places to live tomorrow.

7. **Helping Those with Special Needs** – Community policing stresses exploring new ways to protect and enhance the lives of those who are most vulnerable – juveniles, the elderly, minorities, the poor, the disabled, the homeless. It both assimilates and broadens the scope of previous outreach efforts such as crime prevention and police-community relations.

8. **Grass-Roots Creativity and Support** – Community policing promotes the judicious use of technology, but it also rests on the belief that nothing surpasses what dedicated human beings, talking and working together, can achieve. It invests trust in those who are on the front lines together on the street, relying on their combined judgment, wisdom, and experience to fashion creative new approaches to contemporary community concerns.

9. **Internal Change** – Community policing must be a fully integrated approach that involves everyone in the department, with community policing officers serving as generalists who bridge the gap between the police and the people they serve. The community policing approach plays a crucial role internally by providing information about and awareness of the community and its problems, and by enlisting broad-based community support for the department's overall objectives. Once community policing is accepted as the long-term strategy, all officers should practice it. This could take as long as 10 to 15 years.

10. **Building for the Future** – Community policing provides decentralized, personalized police service to the community. It recognizes that the police cannot impose order on the community from the outside, but that people must be encouraged to think of the police as a resource that they can use in helping to solve contemporary community concerns. It is not a tactic to be applied and then abandoned, but a new philosophy and organizational strategy that provides the flexibility to meet local needs and priorities as they change over time.

APPENDIX B
The Nine Ps of Community Policing

PHILOSOPHY – The community policing philosophy rests on the belief that contemporary challenges require the police to provide full-service policing, proactive and reactive, by involving the community directly as partners in the process of identifying, prioritizing, and solving problems including crime, fear of crime, illicit drugs, social and physical disorder, and neighborhood decay. A department-wide commitment implies changes in policies and procedures.

PERSONALIZED – By providing the community with its own community policing officer, community policing breaks down the anonymity on both sides – community policing officers and community residents know each other on a first-name basis.

POLICING – Community policing maintains a strong law enforcement focus; community policing officers and teams answer calls and make arrests like any other officer, but they also focus on proactive problem solving.

PATROLS – Community policing officers and teams work and patrol their communities, but the goal is to free them from the isolation of the patrol car, often by having them walk the beat or rely on other modes of transportation, such as bicycles, scooters, or horses.

PERMANENT – Community policing rests on assigning community policing officers and teams permanently to defined beats, so that they have the time, opportunity, and continuity to develop the new partnership. Permanence means that community policing officers should not be rotated in and out of their beats, and they should not be used as "fill-ins" for absences and vacations of other personnel.

PLACE – All jurisdictions, no matter how large, ultimately break down into distinct neighborhoods. Community policing decentralizes police officers, often including investigators, so that community policing officers can benefit from "owning" their neighborhood beats in which they can act as a "mini-chief," tailoring the response to the needs and resources of the beat area. Moreover, community policing decentralizes decisionmaking, not only by allowing community policing officers the autonomy and freedom to act, but also by empowering all officers to participate in community-based problem solving.

PROACTIVE – As part of providing full-service policing, community policing balances reactive responses to crime incidents and emergencies with a proactive focus on preventing problems before they occur or escalate.

PARTNERSHIP – Community policing encourages a new partnership between people and their police, which rests on mutual respect, civility, and support.

PROBLEM SOLVING – Community policing redefines the mission of the police to focus on community building and problem solving, so that success or failure depends on qualitative outcomes (problems solved) rather than just on quantitative results (arrests made, citations issued – so-called "numbers policing"). Both quantitative and qualitative measures are necessary.

APPENDIX C
Action Planning

Team Action Task Worksheet

Use this **Action Task Worksheet** to document the **Action Steps** that it will take to achieve the proposed change(s) required to implement community policing. Also include steps necessary to overcome barriers.

NOTE: Groups often find themselves wanting to "back up" – to invite other stakeholders to the table for planning sessions, to enrich the plan by including as many points of view as possible. Therefore you may need to keep revising and adding to your Action Steps/Action Tasks.

Action Step 1: _____

Action Tasks

1. _____
2. _____
3. _____
4. _____
5. _____

Action Step 2: _____

Action Tasks

1. _____
2. _____
3. _____
4. _____
5. _____

Action Step 3: _____

Action Tasks

1. _____
2. _____
3. _____
4. _____
5. _____

Action Step 4: _____

Action Tasks

1. _____
2. _____
3. _____
4. _____
5. _____

Action Step 5: _____

Action Tasks

1. _____
2. _____
3. _____
4. _____
5. _____

Action Step 6: _____

Action Tasks

1. _____
2. _____
3. _____
4. _____
5. _____

Action Step 7: _____

Action Tasks

1. _____
2. _____
3. _____
4. _____
5. _____

TEAM RESPONSE ACTION PLAN FORM

**COMMUNITY POLICING
IMPLEMENTATION**

ACTION PLAN

Action Step/Tasks	Responsible Person	Start/End Dates	Key Stakeholders	Resources/Information Needed
1.				
2.				
3.				
4.				
5.				

Action Planning Checklist

Use this **Action Planning Checklist** to review your work on preparing the **Action Plan**. Go through the questions one by one and review your answers and ideas. When you feel each has been thoroughly answered, move on to the next question. This comprehensive approach will help ensure that all bases are covered.

**Check When Answered
by Team Consensus**

1. Are we satisfied with the overall plan?   _____

2. Are we able to measure results?   _____

3. Will this change contribute to implementing community policing?   _____

4. Have we identified all the **Action Steps/Tasks** that need to be done?   _____

5. Are the **Action Steps/Tasks** in the best sequence?   _____

6. Is someone responsible for each **Action Step/Task**?   _____

7. Have we identified realistic timelines for each action task?   _____

8. Do we have helpful checkpoints and milestones?   _____

9. Have we identified needed resources, and how we will get them?   _____

10. Have we included all stakeholders?   _____

11. Do we have ideas to get these stakeholders and others more involved?   _____

BIBLIOGRAPHY*

Abshire, R. (1995). "Community Policing+Technology=21st Century Policing." *Law Enforcement Technology*, 22(10):42-44, 46-48, 50-52.

Allen, D. & M. Maxfield (1983). "Judging Police Performance: View and Behaviors of Patrol Officers." In R. Bennett (ed.) *Police at Work: Policy Issues and Analysis*. Beverly Hills, CA: Sage Publications.

Alpert, G. & R. Dunham (1989). "Community Policing." In R. Dunham & G. Alpert (eds.) *Critical Issues in Policing: Contemporary Readings*. Prospect Heights, IL: Waveland Press.

Alpert, G. & R. Dunham (1988). *Policing Multi-Ethnic Neighborhoods: The Miami Study and Finding for Law Enforcement in the United States*. New York, NY: Greenwood Press.

Angel, J. (1971). "Toward an Alternative to the Classic Police Organizational Arrangements: A Democratic Model." *Criminology*, 9:186-206.

Baker, T. (1995). "Community Policing: Philosophy or Ideology." *The Chief of Police*, 10(2):39-45.

Banas, D. & R. Trojanowicz (1985). *Uniform Crime Reporting and Community Policing: An Historical Perspective*. East Lansing, MI: Michigan State University, National Neighborhood Foot Patrol Center.

Barnett, C. & R. Bowers (1990). "Community Policing, the New Model for the Way the Police Do Their Job." *Public Management*, 72:2-6.

Bayley, D. (1989). *A Model of Community Policing: The Singapore Force Story*. Washington, DC: National Institute of Justice.

Bazemore, G. & A. Cole (1994). "Police in the Laboratory of the Neighborhood: Evaluating Problem-Oriented Strategies in a Medium-Sized City." *American Journal of Police*, 13(3):119-147.

Belknap, J., M. Morash & R. Trojanowicz (1986). *Implementing a Community Policing Model for Work with Juveniles: An Exploratory Study*. East Lansing, MI: Michigan State University, National Neighborhood Foot Patrol Center.

Bennett, C. (1995). "Followership: An Essential Component of Community Policing." *Police Chief*, 62(9):28, 30, 32.

Bennett, C. (1993). "The Last Taboo of Community Policing." *Police Chief*, 60(8):86.

---

*Developed and maintained by DeVere Woods, who worked closely with the late Robert Trojanowicz as a graduate student in criminal justice.

Bennett, R. & S. Baxter (1985). "Police and Community Participation in Anti-Crime Programs." In J. Fyfe (ed.) *Police Management Today: Issues and Case Studies.* Washington, DC: International City/County Management Association.

Bennett, T. (1994). "Community Policing on the Ground: Developments in Britain." In D. Rosenbaum (ed.) *The Challenge of Community Policing: Testing the Promises.* Thousand Oaks, CA: Sage Publications.

Bennett, T. & R. Kupton (1992). "A National Activity Survey of the Organisation & Use of Community Constables." *British Journal of Criminology,* 32(2):167-182.

Bittner, E. (1970). *The Functions of Police in Modern Society.* Washington, DC: National Institute of Mental Health.

Bittner, E. (1967). "The Police on Skid-Row: A Study of Peace Keeping." *American Sociological Review,* 32:699-715.

Bizzack, J. (1993). "Practical-Centered Policing." *Police Chief,* 60(5):26-29.

Blair, B. (1993). "Promoting Corporate-Community Partnerships." *Police Chief,* 60(12):28-31.

Bobinsky, R. (1994). "Reflections on Community-Oriented Policing." *Law Enforcement Bulletin,* 62(3):15-18.

Bowers, J. & J. Hirsch (1987). "The Impact of Foot Patrol Staffing on Crime and Disorder in Boston: An Unmet Promise." *American Journal of Police,* 6(1):17-44.

Boydstun, J. & M. Sherry (1975). *San Diego Community Profile: Final Report.* Washington, DC: The Police Foundation.

Bradshaw, R. (ed.) (1990). *Reno Police Department's Community Oriented Policing – Plus.* Reno, NV: Reno Police Department.

Braiden, C. (1986). "Bank Robberies and Stolen Bikes." *Canadian Police College Journal,* 10(1).

Brandstatter, A. (1989). *Reinventing the Wheel in Police Work: A Sense of History.* East Lansing, MI: Michigan State University, National Center for Community Policing.

Bright, J. (1991). "Crime Prevention: The British Experience." In K. Stenson & D. Cowell (eds.) *The Politics of Crime Control,* 62-86. London, UK: Sage Publications.

Brown, D. & S. Iles (1985). *Community Constable: A Study of a Policing Initiative.* London, UK: Home Office Research and Planning Unit.

Brown, G. & A. MacNeil (1980). *Police Patrol in Victoria: The Prahran Patrol Evaluation.* Melbourne, Australia: Victoria Police.

Brown, L. (1991). "Community Policing: Its Time Has Come." *Police Chief,* 58(9):6.

Brown, L. (1991). *Policing New York City in the 1990s: The Strategy for Community Policing.* New York, NY: New York City Police Department.

Brown, L. (1989). "Community Policing: A Practical Guide for Police Officers." *Perspectives on Policing,* 12, (NCJ 118001). Washington, DC: National Institute of Justice.

Brown, L. (1985). "Community-Policing Power Sharing." In W. Geller (ed.) *Police Leadership in America: Crisis and Opportunity.* New York, NY: Praeger.

Brown, L. & M. Wycoff (1987). "Policing Houston: Reducing Fear and Improving Service." *Crime & Delinquency,* 33:71-89.

Bucqueroux, B. (1997). *Thinking Strategically about Domestic Violence.* Community Policing Exchange. Washington, DC: Community Policing Consortium.

Bucqueroux, B. (1995). "Community Criminal Justice: Building on the Lessons that Community Policing Teaches." *Topics in Community Corrections*, pp. 9-15, Washington, DC: U.S. Department of Justice, National Institute of Justice.

Bucqueroux, B. (1995). *Community Policing Is Alive and Well.* Community Policing Exchange. Washington, DC: Community Policing Consortium.

Buerger, M. (1994). "The Limits of Community." In D. Rosenbaum (ed.) *The Challenge of Community Policing: Testing the Promises.* Thousands Oaks, CA: Sage Publications.

Buerger, M. (1994). "The Problems of Problem-Solving: Resistance, Interdependencies & Conflicting Interests." *American Journal of Police*, 13(3):1-36.

Buerger, M. (1994). "A Tale of Two Targets: Limitations of Community Anticrime Actions." *Crime & Delinquency*, 40(3):411-436.

Buerger, M. (1993). "The Challenge of Reinventing Police and Community." In D. Weisburd, C. Uchida & L. Green (eds.) *Police Innovation & Control: Problems of Law, Order & Community.* New York, NY: Springer-Verlag.

Bureau of Justice Assistance (1994, August). *Neighborhood-Oriented Policing in Rural Communities: A Program Planning Guide.* Washington, DC: Department of Justice (NCJ 143709).

Bursik, R. & H. Grasmick (1993). *Neighborhoods and Crime: The Dimensions of Effective Community Control.* New York, NY: Macmillan.

Capowich, G. & J. Roehl (1994). "Problem-Oriented Policing: Actions & Effectiveness in San Diego." In D. Rosenbaum (ed.) *The Challenge of Community Policing: Testing the Promises.* Thousands Oaks, CA: Sage Publications.

Chacko, J. & S. Nancoo (eds.) (1993). *Community Policing in Canada.* Toronto, Canada: Canadian Scholars' Press.

Charles Stewart Mott Foundation (1987). *Community Policing: Making the Case for Citizen Involvement.* Flint, MI: Mott Foundation.

Cirel, P., P. Evans, D. McGillis & D. Witcomb (1977). *Community Crime Prevention Program, Seattle, Washington: An Exemplary Project.* Washington, DC: U.S. Department of Justice, National Institute of Justice.

Clairmont, D. (1990). *To the Forefront: Community-Based Zone Policing in Halifax.* Ottawa, Ontario: Canadian Police College, The Royal Canadian Mounted Police.

Clarke, R. (1992). *Situational Crime Prevention: Successful Case Studies.* Albany, NY: Harrow and Heston, Publishers.

Clarke, R. (1983). "Situational Crime Prevention: Its Theoretical Basis and Practical Scope." In M. Tonry & N. Morris (eds.) *Crime and Justice: An Annual Review of Research*, 4. Chicago, IL: University of Chicago Press.

Clarke, R. & D. Cornis (1985). "Modeling Offenders' Decisions: A Framework for Research and Policy." In M. Tonry & N. Morris (eds.) *Crime and Justice: An Annual Review of Research*, 6. Chicago, IL: University of Chicago Press.

Clifton, W. (1987). *Convenience Store Robberies in Gainesville, Florida: An Intervention Strategy by the Gainesville Police Department.* Gainesville, FL: Gainesville Police Department.

Cohen, L. & M. Felson (1979). "Social Change and Crime Rate Trends: A Routine Activity Approach." *American Sociological Review*, 44:588-605.

Community Relations Service (1987). *Principles of Good Policing: Avoiding Violence Between Police and Citizens*. Washington, DC: U.S. Department of Justice.

Connors, E. & B. Webster (1992). *Police, Drugs, and Public Housing*. Research in Brief. Washington, DC: National Institute of Justice.

Cook, L. (1993). "Community Partnerships Increase Resources." *Police Chief*, 60(12):58-63.

Cordner, G. (1995). "Community Policing: Elements & Effectiveness." *Police Forum*, 5(3):1-8.

Cordner, G. (1993). "Getting Serious about Community Involvement." *American Journal of Police*, 12(3):79-88.

Cordner, G. (1988). "A Problem-Oriented Approach to Community-Oriented Policing." In J. Greene & S. Mastrofski (eds.) *Community Policing: Rhetoric or Reality*. New York, NY: Praeger.

Cordner, G. (1986). "Fear of Crime and the Police: An Evaluation of a Fear-Reduction Strategy." *Journal of Police Science and Administration*, 14:223-233.

Cordner, G. (1985). *The Baltimore County Citizen Oriented Police Enforcement (COPE) Project: Final Evaluation*. Final report to the Florence V. Burden Foundation. Baltimore, MD: Criminal Justice Department, University of Baltimore.

Cordner, G., O. Marenin & J. Murphy (1986). "Police Responsiveness to Community Norms." *American Journal of Police*, 5(2):83-107.

Cordner, G. & G. Williams (1995). "The CALEA Standards. What is the Fit with Community Policing?" *National Institute of Justice Journal*, 229:39-40, (387-164/44305).

Couper, D. & S. Lobitz (1991). "The Customer is Always Right: Applying Vision, Leadership and Problem-Solving Methods to Community Policing." *Police Chief*, 58:16-23.

Couper, D. & S. Lobitz (1991). *Quality Policing: The Madison Experience*. Washington, DC: Police Executive Research Forum.

Cox, J. (1992). "Small Departments and Community Policing." *Law Enforcement Bulletin*, 61(212):1-4.

Cronin, R. (1994). *Innovative Community Partnerships: Working Together for Change*. Washington, DC: Police Executive Research Forum.

Currie, E. (1985). *Confronting Crime: An American Challenge*. New York, NY: Pantheon Books.

Cutliffe, M. (1994). "Community Policing & Residential Traffic Control." *Law Enforcement Bulletin*, 63(8):12-14.

Dantzker, G., A. Lurigio, S. Harnett, S. Houmes, S. Davidsdottir & K. Donovan (1995). "Preparing Police Officers for Community Policing: An Evaluation of Training for Chicago's Alternative Policing Strategy." *Police Studies*, 18(1):45-69.

Davis, R. (1985). "Organizing the Community for Improving Policing." In W. Geller (ed.) *Police Leadership in America: Crisis and Opportunity*. New York, NY: Praeger.

Doone, P. (1989). "Potential Impacts of Community Policing on Criminal Investigation Strategies." In W. Young & N. Cameron (eds.) *Effectiveness and Change in Policing. Study Series 33*. Wellington, New Zealand: Institute of Criminology, Victoria University of Wellington.

Eck, J. (1990). "A Realistic Local Approach to Controlling Drug Harm." *Public Management*, 72(6):7-12.

Eck, J. (1989). *Police and Drug Control: A Home Field Advantage*. Washington, DC: Police Executive Research Forum.

Eck, J. & D. Rosenbaum (1994). "The New Police Orders: Effectiveness, Equity & Efficiency in Community Policing." In D. Rosenbaum (ed.) *The Challenge of Community Policing: Testing the Promises*. Thousand Oaks, CA: Sage Publications.

Eck, J. & W. Spelman (1989). "A Problem-Oriented Approach to Police Service Delivery." In D. Kenney (ed.) *Police and Policing: Contemporary Issues*. New York, NY: Praeger.

Eck, J. & W. Spelman (1987). *Problem Solving: Problem-Oriented Policing in Newport News*. Washington, DC: Police Executive Research Forum.

Eck, J. & W. Spelman (1987). "Who Ya Gonna Call? The Police as Problem Busters." *Crime & Delinquency*, 33:31-52.

Eck, J. & G. Williams (1991). "Criminal Investigations." In W. Geller (ed.) *Local Government Police Management*. Washington, DC: International City/County Management Association.

Ent, C. & J. Hendricks (1991). "Bicycle Patrol: A Community Policing Alternative." *Police Chief*, 58:58-60.

Esbensen, F. (1987). "Foot Patrol: Of What Value?" *American Journal of Police*, 6(1):45-66.

Farmer, M. (ed.) (1981). *Differential Police Response Strategies*. Washington, DC: Police Executive Research Forum.

Farrell, M. (1988). "The Development of the Community Patrol Officer Program: Community-Oriented Policing." In J. Greene & S. Mastrofski (eds.) *Community Policing: Rhetoric or Reality*. New York, NY: Praeger.

Fay, B. (1984). *Social Theory and Political Practice*. London, UK: George Allen & Unwin Publishers Ltd.

Fielding, N. (1995). *Community Policing*. Oxford, UK: Clarendon Press.

Fielding, N., C. Kemp & C. Norris (1989). "Constraints on the Practice of Community Policing." In D. Smith & R. Morgan (eds.) *Coming to Terms with Policing*. London, UK: Routledge.

Fisher, B. (1993). "What Works: Blockwatch Meetings or Crime Prevention Seminars?" *Journal of Crime & Justice*, 16(1):1-27.

Fowler, F., M. McCalla & T. Mangione (1979). *Reducing Crime and Fear in the Urban Residential Area: The Planning and Evaluation of an Integrated Approach to Opportunity Reduction*. Boston, MA: Survey Research Program, University of Massachusetts.

Fowler, F. & T. Mangione (1983). *Neighborhood Crime, Fear and Social Control: A Second Look at the Hartford Program*. Washington, DC: U.S. Government Printing Office.

Freeman, M. (1989). *Community-Oriented Policing*. MIS Report, International City/County Management Association, 24:9.

Friedmann, R. (1987). "Citizens' Attitudes Toward the Police: Results from Experiment in Community Policing in Israel." *American Journal of Police*, 6(1):67-94.

Fulton, R. (1993). "Community Policing on Horseback." *Law Enforcement Technology*, 20(5):32.

Gaines, L. (1994). "Community-Oriented Policing: Management Issues, Concerns & Problems." *Journal of Contemporary Criminal Justice*, 10(1):19-35.

Geller, W. & G. Swanger (1995). *Managing Innovations in Policing: The Untapped Potential of the Middle Manager*. Washington, DC: Police Executive Research Forum.

George, A. (1992). "The First Line Supervisor's Perspective of Community Policing: A Participant Observation Study." Unpublished paper for master's of science degree, Michigan State University, East Lansing, Michigan.

Glensor, R. & K. Pewak (1996). "Implementing Change: Community-Oriented Policing & Problem Solving." *Law Enforcement Bulletin*, 65(7):14-21.

Goldstein, H. (1990). *Problem-Oriented Policing*. New York, NY: McGraw Hill.

Goldstein, H. (1987). "Toward Community-Oriented Policing: Potential, Basic Requirements, and Threshold Question." *Crime & Delinquency*, 33:6-30.

Goldstein, H. (1979). "Improving Policing: A Problem-Oriented Approach." *Crime & Delinquency*, 25:236-258.

Goldstein, H. (1977). *Policing a Free Society*. Cambridge, MA: Ballinger.

Goldstein, H. & C. Susmilch (1982). *Experimenting with the Problem-Oriented Approach to Improving Police Service: A Report and Some Reflections on Two Case Studies*. Madison, WI: Law School, University of Wisconsin.

Goldstein, H. & C. Susmilch (1982). *The Repeat Sexual Offender in Madison: A Memorandum on the Problem and the Community's Response*. Madison, WI: Law School, University of Wisconsin.

Goldstein, H. & C. Susmilch (1981). *The Problem-Oriented Approach to Improving Police Service: A Description of the Project and an Elaboration of the Concept*. Madison, WI: Law School, University of Wisconsin.

Goldstein, H., C. Susmilch, C. Marlaire & M. Scott (1981). *The Drinking-Driver in Madison: A Study of the Problem and the Community's Response*. Madison, WI: Law School, University of Wisconsin.

Greenberg, S., W. Rohe & J. Williams (1985). *Informal Citizen Action and Crime Prevention at the Neighborhood Level: Synthesis and Assessment of the Research*. Washington, DC: U.S. Government Printing Office.

Greenberg, S., W. Rohe & J. Williams (1982). *Safe and Secure Neighborhoods: Physical Characteristics and Informal Territorial Control in High and Low Crime Neighborhoods*. Washington, DC: U.S. Government Printing Office.

Greene, H. (1993). "Community-Oriented Policing in Florida." *American Journal of Police*, 12(3):141-155.

Greene, J. (1989). "Police Officer Job Satisfaction and Community Perceptions: Implications for Community-Oriented Policing." *Journal of Research in Crime & Delinquency*, 16:168-184.

Greene, J. (1987). "Foot Patrol and Community Policing: Past Practice and Future Prospects." *American Journal of Police*, 6(1):1-16.

Greene, J., W. Bergman & E. McLaughlin (1994). "Implementing Community Policing: Cultural Change in Police Organizations." In D. Rosenbaum (ed.) *The Challenge of Policing: Testing the Promises*. Thousand Oaks, CA: Sage Publications.

Greene, J. & S. Mastrofski (eds.) (1988). *Community Policing: Rhetoric or Reality*. New York, NY: Praeger.

Greene, J. & R. Taylor (1988). "Community-Based Policing and Foot Patrol: Issues of Theory and Evaluation." In J. Greene & S. Mastrofski (eds.) *Community Policing: Rhetoric or Reality*. New York, NY: Praeger.

Grinc, R. (1994). "Angels in Marble: Problems in Stimulating Community Involvement in Community Policing." *Crime & Delinquency*, 40(3):437-468.

Gruber, C. (1993). "Elgin's Residential Officer Program Makes a Difference." *Police Chief*, 60(5):30-32, 37.

Guyot, D. (1991). "Problem-Oriented Policing Shines in the Stats." *PM: Public Management*, 73(9):12-16.

Hamilton, S.W. (1993). "Community Policing: The Saskatoon Experience." *Law & Order*, 41(12):20-26.

Harrison, B. (1994). "Integrating the Focus of Law Enforcement's Future." *Police Chief*, 61(1):20-26.

Harrison, S. (1996). "Quality Policing & the Challenges for Leadership." *Police Chief*, 61(1):52-61.

Hartmann, F. (ed.) (1988). "Debating the Evolution of American Policing." *Perspectives on Policing*, 5, (NCJ 114214). Washington DC: National Institute of Justice.

Hartmann, F., L. Brown & D. Stephens (1988). *Community Policing: Would You Know it if You Saw it?* East Lansing, MI: Michigan State University, National Neighborhood Foot Patrol Center.

Hatry, H. & J. Greiner (1986). *Improving the Use of Management by Objectives in Police Departments*. Washington, DC: Urban Institute.

Hatry, H. & J. Greiner (1986). *Improving the Use of Quality Circles in Police Departments*. Washington, DC: Urban Institute.

Hayeslip, D. & G. Cordner (1987). "The Effects of Community-Oriented Patrol on Police Officer Attitudes." *American Journal of Police*, 6(1):95-119.

Higdon, R. & P. Huber (1987). *How to Fight Fear: The Citizen Oriented Police Enforcement Program Package*. Washington, DC: Police Executive Research Forum.

Hoare, M., G. Stewart & C. Purcell (1984). *The Problem-Oriented Approach: Four Pilot Studies*. London, UK: Metropolitan Police, Management Services Department.

Holland, L. (1985). "Police and the Community: The Detroit Administration Experience." *FBI Law Enforcement Bulletin*, 54:1-6.

Hoover, L. & E. Mader (1990). "Attitudes of Police Chiefs Toward Private Sector Management Principles." *American Journal of Police*, 9:25-38.

Horne, P. (1991). "Not Just Old Wine in New Bottles: The Inextricable Relationship Between Crime Prevention and Community Policing." *Police Chief*, 58:24-30.

Hornick, J., B. Burrows, D. Phillips & B. Leighton (1993). *An Evaluation of the Neighborhood Foot Patrol Program of the Edmonton Police Service*. Edmonton, Alberta: Canadian Research Institute for Law and the Family.

Hornick, J., B. Burrows, I. Tjosvold & D. Phillips (1989). *An Evaluation of the Neighborhood Foot Patrol Program of the Edmonton Police Service*. Edmonton, Alberta: Canadian Research Institute for Law and the Family.

Howard, K. (1993). "Alexandria Establishes Residential Officer Program." *Police Chief*, 60(5):38.

International City/County Management Association (1992). "Community-Oriented Policing: An Alternative Strategy." *Source Book*. Washington, DC: International City/County Management Association.

Jackson, E. (1992). "Campus Police Embrace Community-Based Approach." *Police Chief*, 59(12):63-64.

Jacobs, J. (1961). *The Death and Life of Great American Cities*. New York, NY: Vintage.

Jeffrey, C. (1971). *Crime Prevention Through Environmental Design*. Beverly Hills, CA: Sage Publications.

Johnson, P. (1984). "Police Community Relations: The Management Factor." *American Journal of Police*, 3:185-203.

Jones, L. (1989). "Community-Oriented Policing." *Law and Order*, 37:25-27.

Joseph, T. (1994). "Walking the Minefield of Community-Oriented Policing." *Law Enforcement Bulletin*, 63(9):8-12.

Karchmer, C. & J. Eck (1991). "Drug Control." In W. Geller (ed.) *Local Government Police Management*. Washington, DC: International City/County Management Association.

Kelling, G. (1988). "Police and Communities: The Quiet Revolution." *Perspectives on Policing*, 1, (NCJ 109955). Washington, DC: National Institute of Justice.

Kelling, G. (1987). "Acquiring a Taste for Order: The Community and the Police." *Crime & Delinquency*, 33:90-102.

Kelling, G. (1985). "Order Maintenance, the Quality of Urban Life, and Police: A Line of Argument." In W. Geller (ed.) *Police Leadership in America: Crisis and Opportunity*. New York, NY: Praeger.

Kelling, G. (1981). "Conclusions." In *The Newark Foot Patrol Experiment*. Washington, DC: The Police Foundation.

Kelling, G. & M. Moore (1988). "The Evolving Strategy of Policing." *Perspectives on Policing*, 4. Washington, DC: National Institute of Justice.

Kelling, G. & J. Stewart (1989). "Neighborhoods and Police: The Maintenance of Civil Authority." *Perspectives on Policing*, 10, (NCJ 115950). Washington, DC: National Institute of Justice.

Kelling, G., R. Wasserman & H. Williams (1988). "Police Accountability and Community Policing." *Perspectives on Policing*, 7, (NCJ 114211). Washington, DC: National Institute of Justice.

Kelling, G. & M. Wycoff (1991). "Implementing Community Policing: The Administrative Problem." Paper prepared for the Executive Session on Policing Program in Criminal Justice Policy and Management. John F. Kennedy School of Government, Harvard University.

Kennedy, D. (1993). "The Strategic Management of Police Resources." *Perspectives on Policing*, 14, (NCJ 139565). Washington, DC: National Institute of Justice.

Kime, R. (1995). "Where Does the COPS Program Stand?" *Police Chief*, 62(8):8, 10.

King, D. (1991). "Managing for Excellence." *FBI Law Enforcement Bulletin*, 60:20-21.

Klockars, C. (1988). "The Rhetoric of Community Policing." In J. Greene & S. Mastrofski (eds.) *Community Policing: Rhetoric or Reality*. New York, NY: Praeger.

Klockars, C. (1985). "Order Maintenance, the Quality of Urban Life, and Police: A Different Line of Argument." In W. Geller (ed.) *Police Leadership in America: Crisis and Opportunity*. New York, NY: Praeger.

Kobrin, S. & L. Schuerman (1983). *Crime and Changing Neighborhoods: Executive Summary*. Los Angeles, CA: Social Science Research Institute, University of Southern California.

Kratcoski, S. & D. Dukes (1995). *Issues in Community Policing*. Cincinnati, OH: Anderson Publishing Co.

Kuykendall, J. & R. Roberg (1982). "Mapping Police Organizational Change." *Criminology*, 20:241-256.

Larson, R. (1990). *Rapid Response and Community Policing: Are They Really in Conflict?* East Lansing, MI: Michigan State University, National Center for Community Policing.

Larson, R. (1989). "The New Crime Stoppers." *Technology Review*, 92:26-31.

Lavrakas, P. (1985). "Citizen Self-Help and Neighborhood Crime Prevention Policy." In L. Curtis (ed.) *American Violence and Public Policy*. New Haven, CT: Yale University Press.

Lavrakas, P., S. Bennett & B. Fisher (1987). "The Neighborhood Anti-Crime Self-Help Program Evaluation: Some Preliminary Findings on Community Organization and Police Interaction." A paper presented at the annual meeting of the American Society of Criminology.

Lavrakas, P. & J. Kushmuk (1986). "Evaluating Crime Prevention Through Environmental Design: The Portland Commercial Demonstration Project." In D. Rosenbaum (ed.) *Community Crime Prevention: Does it Work?* Beverly Hills, CA: Sage Publications.

Law Enforcement Assistance Administration (1973). *National Advisory Commission on Criminal Justice Standards and Goals*. Washington, DC: Department of Justice.

Leighton, B. (1994). "Community Policing in Canada: An Overview of Experience & Evaluation." In D. Rosenbaum (ed.) *The Challenge of Community Policing: Testing the Promises*. Thousands Oaks, CA: Sage Publications.

Leighton, B. (1991). "Visions of Community Policing: Rhetoric & Reality in Canada." *Canadian Journal of Criminology*, 33(3-4):485-522.

Lewis, D. & G. Salem (1985). *Fear of Crime: Incivility and the Production of a Social Problem*. New Brunswick, NJ: Transaction Books.

Loree, D. (1988). "Innovation and Change in a Regional Police Force." *Canadian Police College Journal*, 12:205-239.

Lurigio, A. & W. Skogan (1994). *Planning Report for the Experimental Police District*. Madison, WI: Madison Police Department.

Madison Police Department (1988). *Planning Report for the Experimental Police District*. Madison, WI: Madison Police Department.

Manning, P. (1989). "Community Policing." In R. Dunham & G. Alpert (eds.) *Critical Issues in Policing*. Prospect Heights, IL: Waveland Press.

Manning, P. (1988). "Community Policing as a Drama of Control." In J. Greene & S. Mastrofski (eds.) *Community Policing: Rhetoric or Reality*. New York, NY: Praeger.

Manning, P. (1984). "Community Policing." *American Journal of Police*, 3:205-227.

Marenin, O. (1989). "The Utility of Community Needs Surveys in Community Policing." *Police Studies*, 12:73-81.

Marx, G. (1989). "Commentary: Some Trends and Issues in Citizen Involvement in the Law Enforcement Process." *Crime & Delinquency*, 35:500-519.

Mastrofski, S. (1996). *Law Enforcement in a Time of Community Policing.* Washington, DC: National Institute of Justice, Department of Justice,

Mastrofski, S. (1993). "Varieties of Community Policing." *American Journal of Police*, 123:65-77.

Mastrofski, S. (1992). "What Does Community Policing Mean for Daily Police Work?" *National Institute of Justice Journal*, 225:23-27.

Mastrofski, S. (1988). "Community Policing as Reform: A Cautionary Tale." In J. Greene & S. Mastrofski (eds.) *Community Policing: Rhetoric or Reality*. New York, NY: Praeger.

Mastrofski, S. (1983). "Police Knowledge of the Patrol Beat: A Performance Measure." In R. Bennett (ed.) *Police at Work: Policy Issues and Analysis*. Beverly Hills, CA: Sage Publications.

Mastrofski, S. & J. Greene (1993). "Community and the Rule of Law." In D. Weisburd, C. Uchida & L. Green (eds.) *Police Innovation & Control of the Police: Problems of Law, Order & Community*. New York, NY: Springer-Verlag.

McElroy, J., C. Cosgrove & S. Sadd (1993). *Community Policing: The CPOP in New York*. Newbury Park, CA: Sage Publications.

McElroy, J., C. Cosgrove & S. Sadd (1989). "An Examination of the Community Patrol Officer Program (CPOP) in New York City." An unpublished report by the Vera Institute of Justice, New York.

McKnight, J. (n.d.). *The Future of Low-Income Neighborhoods and the People Who Reside There: A Capacity-Oriented Strategy for Neighborhood Development*. Flint, MI: Charles Stewart Mott Foundation.

Meese, E. (1991). "Community Policing and the Police Officer." A paper prepared for the Executive Session on Policing Program in Criminal Justice Policy and Management. John F. Kennedy School of Government, Harvard University.

Melancon, D. (1984). "Quality Circles: The Shape of Things to Come?" *Police Chief*, 51:54-56.

Miller, L. & K. Hess (1994). *Community Policing: Theory & Practice*. St. Paul, MN: West Publishing.

Ministry of the Solicitor General (1990, Jan.). *Community Policing: Shaping the Future*. Toronto, Ontario: Queen's Printer of Ontario.

Mitchell, W. (1990). "Problem-Oriented Policing and Drug Enforcement in Newport News." *Public Management*, 72:13-16.

Moore, M. (1994). "Research Synthesis & Policy Implications." In D. Rosenbaum (ed.) *The Challenge of Community Policing: Testing the Promises*. Thousand Oaks, CA: Sage Publications.

Moore, M. (1992). "Problem Solving and Community Policing." In M. Tonry & N. Morris (eds.) *Modern Policing, Crime & Justice: A Review of Research*, Volume 15. Chicago, IL: University of Chicago Press.

Moore, M. & G. Kelling (1983). "To Serve and Protect: Learning From Police History." *The Public Interest*, 70.

Moore, M. & M. Kleiman (1989). "The Police and Drugs." *Perspectives on Policing*, 11. Washington DC: National Institute of Justice.

Moore, M. & D. Stephens (1991). *Beyond Command and Control: The Strategic Management of Police Departments*. Washington, DC: Police Executive Research Forum.

Moore, M. & R. Trojanowicz (1988). "Corporate Strategies for Policing." *Perspectives on Policing*, 6, (NCJ 114215). Washington DC: National Institute of Justice.

Moore, M. & R. Trojanowicz (1988). "Policing and the Fear of Crime." *Perspectives on Policing*, 3, (NCJ 111459). Washington DC: National Institute of Justice.

Moore, M., R. Trojanowicz & G. Kelling (1989). "Crime and Policing." In J. Fyfe (ed.) *Police Practices in the '90's: Key Management Issues*, 31-54. Washington DC: International City Management Association. Also in *Perspectives on Policing*, 2. Washington DC: National Institute of Justice.

Murphy, C. (1990, Jan). "Problem-Oriented Policing." In Ministry of the Solicitor General (ed.) *Community Policing: Shaping the Future*. Toronto, Ontario: Queen's Printer for Ontario.

Murphy, C. (1988). "The Development, Impact, and Implications of Community Policing in Canada." In J. Greene & S. Mastrofski (eds.) *Community Policing: Rhetoric or Reality*. New York, NY: Praeger.

Murphy, C. & G. Muir (1985). *Community-Based Policing: A Review of the Critical Issues*. Ottawa, Ontario: Solicitor General of Canada.

National Institute of Justice (1996). *National Institute of Justice Journal*, 231 (405-034/54321). Washington, DC: U.S. Government Printing Office.

National Institute of Justice (1995). *Managing Innovation in Policing. The Untapped Potential of the Middle Manager*. Research Preview. Washington, DC: U.S. Department of Justice.

National Institute of Justice (1992). *Community Policing in Seattle: A Model Partnership Between Citizens and Police*. Research in Brief (NCJ 136608). Washington, DC: National Institute of Justice.

National Institute of Justice (1992, August). "Community Policing." *National Institute of Justice Journal*.

New York City Police Department (1988). *Community Patrol Officer Program: Problem-Solving Guide*. New York, NY: New York City Police Department.

Nielsen, R. & B. Steele (1984). "Quality Circles: A Police Management Experiment." *Police Chief*, 51:52-53.

Norman, M. (1984). "Quality Circles: A Program to Improve Employee Attitudes and the Quality of Series." *Police Chief*, 51:46-49.

Normandeau, A. (1993). "Community Policing in Canada: A Review of Some Recent Studies." *American Journal of Police*, 12(1):57-73.

Oettmeier, T. & W. Bieck (1989). *Integrating Investigative Operations Through Neighborhood Oriented Policing: Executive Session #2*. Houston, TX: Houston Police Department.

Oettmeier, T. & W. Bieck (1987). *Developing a Police Style for Neighborhood Oriented Policing: Executive Session #1*. Houston, TX: Houston Police Department.

Oettmeier, T. & L. Brown (1988). "Developing a Neighborhood-Oriented Policing Style." In J. Greene & S. Mastrofski (eds.) *Community Policing: Rhetoric or Reality*. New York, NY: Praeger.

Office of Juvenile Justice & Delinquency Prevention (1995). *Matrix of Community-Based Initiatives: Program Descriptions* (387-167/20011). Washington, DC: U.S. Government Printing Office.

Osborn, R. (1980). "Policing in Tune with Society." *Police Studies*, 3:30-36.

Osborne, D & T. Gaebler (1992). *Reinventing Government: How the Entrepreneurial Spirit Is Transforming the Public Sector*. New York, NY: Plume Publishing.

Ostrom, E., R. Parks & G. Whitaker (1978). "Police Agency Size: Some Evidence on its Effects." *Police Studies*, 1:34-46.

Owens, R. (n.d.). *COPS: Community Oriented Problem Solving*. Oxnard, CA: Oxnard Police Department.

Parker, P. (1991). "Herman Goldstein: The Man Who Made Problem-Oriented Policing a Reality." *Police*, 15:10-12, 75.

Parker, P. (1990). "POP vs. Drugs." *Police*, 14:34-37.

Pate, A. (1989). "Community-Oriented Policing in Baltimore." In D. Kenney (ed.) *Police and Policing: Contemporary Issues*. New York, NY: Praeger.

Pate, A. & P. Shtull (1994). "Community Policing Grows in Brooklyn: An Inside View of the New York Police Department's Model Precinct." *Crime & Delinquency*, 40(3):384-410.

Pate, A., M. Wycoff, W. Skogan & L. Sherman (1989). *Reducing Fear of Crime in Houston and Newark: A Summary Report*. Washington, DC: The Police Foundation.

Pate, A., M. Wycoff, W. Skogan & L. Sherman (1986). *Reducing Fear of Crime in Houston and Newark: A Summary Report*. Washington, DC: The Police Foundation.

Patterson, J. (1995). "Community Policing: Lessons of History." *Law Enforcement Bulletin*, 64(1):5-10.

Payne, D. & R. Trojanowicz (1985). *Performance Profiles of Foot versus Motor Officers*. East Lansing, MI: Michigan State University, National Neighborhood Foot Patrol Center.

Peak, K. (1994). "Police Executives as Agents of Change." *Police Chief*, 61(1):27-29.

Philadelphia Police Study Task Force (1987). *Philadelphia and its Police: Toward a New Partnership*. Philadelphia, PA: Philadelphia Police Study Task Force.

Police Executive Research Forum (1996). *Themes & Variations in Community Policing: Case Studies of Community Policing*. Washington, DC: Police Executive Research Forum.

Police Executive Research Forum (n.d.). *The Key Elements of Problem-Oriented Policing*. Washington, DC: Police Executive Research Forum.

Police Executive Research Forum (1989). *Taking a Problem-Oriented Approach to Drugs: An Interim Report*. Washington, DC: Police Executive Research Forum.

The Police Foundation (1981). *The Newark Foot Patrol Experiment*. Washington, DC: The Police Foundation.

Poyner, B. (1980). *Street Attacks and their Environmental Settings*. London, UK: Tavistock Institute of Human Relations.

Radelet, L. (1986). *The Police and the Community*, Fourth Edition. New York, NY: Macmillan Publishing.

Ramsay, M. (1982). *City-Centre Crime: The Scope for Situational Prevention*. Research and Planning Unit Paper 10. London, UK: Home Office.

Redlinger, L. (1994). "Community Policing & Changes in the Organizational Structure." *Journal of Contemporary Criminal Justice*, 10(1):36-58.

Reinier, G., M. Greenlee & M. Gibbens (n.d.). *Crime Analysis in Support of Patrol*. National Evaluation Program: Phase I Report. Washington, DC: U.S. Government Printing Office.

Reiss, A. (1985). "Shaping and Serving the Community: The Role of the Police Chief Executive." In W. Geller (ed.) *Police Leadership in America: Crisis and Opportunity*. New York, NY: Praeger.

Reiss, A. & M. Tonry (eds.) (1986). *Communities and Crime*. Crime and Justice, 8. Chicago, IL: University of Chicago Press.

Riechers, L. & R. Roberg (1990). "Community Policing: A Critical Review of Underlying Assumptions." *Journal of Police Science and Administration*, 17(2):105-114.

Roberg, R. (1994). "Can Today's Police Organizations Effectively Implement Community Policing?" In D. Rosenbaum (ed.) *The Challenge of Community Policing: Testing the Promises*. Thousand Oaks, CA: Sage Publications.

Rosenbaum, D. (1994). *The Challenge of Community Policing: Testing the Promises*. Thousand Oaks, CA: Sage Publications.

Rosenbaum, D. (1989). "Community Crime Prevention: A Review of What is Known." In D. Kenney (ed.) *Police and Policing: Contemporary Issues*. New York, NY: Praeger.

Rosenbaum, D. (ed.) (1989). *Community Crime Prevention: Does it Work?* Beverly Hills, CA: Sage Publications.

Rosenbaum, D. (1987). "The Theory and Research Behind Neighborhood Watch: Is it a Sound Fear and Crime Reduction Strategy?" *Crime & Delinquency*, 33:103-134.

Rosenbaum, D. & T. Baumer (1981). *Measuring Fear of Crime: A Set of Recommended Scales*. Evanston, IL: Westinghouse Evaluation Institute.

Rosenbaum, D. & L. Heath (1990). "The 'Psycho-Logic' of Fear-Reduction and Crime-Prevention Programs." In J. Edwards, R. Tindale, L. Heath & E. Posavac (eds.) *Social Influence Processes and Prevention. Social Psychological Applications to Social Issues—Volume I*. New York, NY: Plenum Press.

Rosenbaum, D., D. Lewis & J. Grant (1985). *The Impact of Community Crime Prevention Programs in Chicago: Can Neighborhood Organizations Make a Difference?* Final report to the Ford Foundation. Chicago, IL: Department of Criminal Justice, University of Illinois.

Rosenbaum, D., S. Yeh & D. Wilkinson (1994). "Impact of Community Policing on Police Personnel: A Quasi-Experimental Test." *Crime & Delinquency*, 40(3):331-353.

Ryan, J. (1994). "Community Policing: Trends, Policies, Programs & Definitions." In A. Roberts (ed.) *Critical Issues in Crime & Justice*. Thousand Oaks, CA: Sage Publications.

Sadd, S. & R. Grinc (1996). *Implementation Challenges in Community Policing: Innovative Neighborhood-Oriented Policing in Eight Cities*. Research in Brief (NCJ 157932). Washington, DC: National Institute of Justice, U.S. Department of Justice.

Sadd, S. & R. Grinc (1994). "Innovative Neighborhood Oriented Policing: An Evaluation in Eight Cities." In D. Rosenbaum (ed.) *The Challenge of Community Policing: Testing the Promises*. Thousand Oaks, CA: Sage Publications.

Schwartz, A. & S. Clarren (1977). *The Cincinnati Team Policing Experiment: A Summary Report*. Washington, DC: The Police Foundation.

Sensenbrenner, J. (1986). "Quality Comes to City Hall." *Harvard Business Review*, March-April.

Sherman, L. (1989). "Repeat Calls for Service: Policing the 'Hot Spots.'" In D. Kenney (ed.) *Police and Policing: Contemporary Issues.* New York, NY: Praeger.

Sherman, L. (1986). "Policing Communities: What Works?" In A. Reiss & M. Tonry (eds.) *Communities and Crime, Crime and Justice Annual*, Volume 8. Chicago, IL: University of Chicago Press.

Sherman, L. & R. Berk (1984). "The Specific Deterrent Effects of Arrest for Domestic Assault." *American Sociological Review*, 49(2):261-272.

Sherman, L., P. Gartin & M. Buerger (1989). "Hot Spots of Predatory Crime: Routine Activities and the Criminology of Place." *Criminology*, 27:27-55.

Sherman, L., C. Milton & T. Kelly (1973). *Team Policing: Seven Case Studies*. Washington, DC: The Police Foundation.

Sill, P. (1991). "Community-Oriented Policing and Crime Prevention Training: A Must for the '90s." *Police Chief*, 58(11), pp. 56-57.

Skogan, W. (1995). *Community Policing in Chicago: Year Two*. NIJ Research Preview.

Skogan, W. (1994) "The Impact of Community Policing on Neighborhood Residents: A Cross-Site Analysis." In D. Rosenbaum (ed.) *The Challenge of Community Policing: Testing the Promises*. Thousand Oaks, CA: Sage Publications.

Skogan, W. (1990). *Disorder and Decline: Crime and the Spiral of Decay in American Neighborhoods*. New York, NY: Free Press.

Skogan, W. (1987). "The Impact of Victimization on Fear." *Crime & Delinquency*, 33:135-154.

Skolnick, J. (1973). "The Police and the Urban Ghetto." In A. Niederhoffer & A. Blumberg (eds.) *The Ambivalent Force: Perspective on the Police*. San Francisco, CA: Rinehart Press.

Skolnick, J. & D. Bayley (1988). *Community Policing: Issues and Practice Around the World*. Washington, DC: National Institute of Justice.

Skolnick, J. & D. Bayley (1988). "Theme and Variation in Community Policing." In M. Tonry & N. Morris (eds.) *Crime and Justice: A Review of Research*, Volume 8. Chicago, IL: University of Chicago Press.

Skolnick, J. & D. Bayley (1986). *The New Blue Line: Police Innovations in Six American Cities*. New York, NY: Free Press.

Skolnick, J. & R. Leo (1992). "The Ethics of Deceptive Interrogations." *Criminal Justice Ethics*, pp. 3-12.

Sloan, R., R. Trojanowicz & B. Bucqueroux (1992). *Basic Issues in Training: A Foundation for Community Policing*. East Lansing, MI: National Center for Community Policing Publishing.

Sower, C. (1957). *Community Involvement*. Glencoe, IL: Free Press.

Sparrow, M. (1993). "Information Systems and the Development of Policing." *Perspectives on Policing*, 16, (NCS 139306). Washington, DC: National Institute of Justice.

Sparrow, M. (1992). "Integrating Distinct Management Styles: The Challenge for Police Leadership." *American Journal of Police*, 12(2):1-16.

Sparrow, M. (1988). "Implementing Community Policing." *Perspectives on Policing*, 9, (NCJ 114217). Washington, DC: National Institute of Justice.

Sparrow, M., M. Moore & D. Kennedy (1990). *Beyond 911*. New York, NY: Basic Books.

Spelman, W. & J. Eck (1989). "The Police and Delivery of Local Governmental Services: A Problem Oriented Approach." In J. Fyfe (ed.) *Police Practices in the '90s: Key Management Issues*, pp. 55-72. Washington, DC: International City/County Management Association.

Spelman, W. & J. Eck (1989). "Sitting Ducks, Ravenous Wolves, and Helping Hands: New Approaches to Urban Policing." Public Affairs Comment. Austin, TX: Lyndon Johnson School of Public Affairs, University of Texas, Austin.

Spelman, W. & J. Eck (1987). "Problem-Oriented Policing." Research in Brief, January. Washington, DC: National Institute of Justice.

Spelman, W. & J. Eck (1987). "Problem-Oriented Policing Bureaucracy." A paper presented to the annual meeting of the American Political Science Association.

Spergel, I. (1969). *Community Problem-Solving*. Chicago, IL: University of Chicago Press.

Stern, G. & P. Still (1991). "Community Policing Six Years Later: What Have We Learned." *Law and Order*, 39:52-54.

Strecher, V. (1991). "Revising the Histories & Futures of Policing." Reprinted in V. Kappeler (ed.) *The Police & Society: Touch Stone Readings* (1994). Prospect Heights, IL: Waveland Press.

Sunahara, D. (1991). "Implementing Community Policing." In D. Orgle (ed.) *Strategic Planning for Police*. Ottawa Canadian Police College.

Sykes, G. (1994). "Accreditation & Community Policing: Passing Fads or Basic Reforms?" *Journal of Contemporary Criminal Justice*, 10(1):1-16.

Sykes, G. (1986). "Street Justice: A Moral Defense of Order Maintenance Policing." *Justice Quarterly*, 3:497-512.

Tafoya, W. (1990). "The Future of Policing." *FBI Law Enforcement Bulletin*, 59(1):13-17.

Taft, P. (1986). *Fighting Fear: The Baltimore County COPE Project*. Washington, DC: Police Executive Research Forum.

Talarico, S. & C. Swanson, Jr. (1980). "The Limits of Team Policing?" *Police Studies*, 3:21-29.

Taub, R., D. Taylor & J. Dunham (1984). *Patterns of Neighborhood Change: Race and Crime in Urban America*. Chicago, IL: University of Chicago Press.

Taub, R., D. Taylor & J. Dunham (1982). *Crime, Fear of Crime, and the Deterioration of Urban Neighborhoods: Executive Summary*. Washington, DC: U.S. Government Printing Office.

Taylor, R., S. Gottfredson & S. Bower (1980). "The Defensibility of Defensible Space." In T. Hirschi & M. Gottfredson (eds.) *Understanding Crime*. Beverly Hills, CA: Sage Publications.

Taylor, R., S. Gottfredson & S. Schumaker (1984). *Neighborhood Response to Disorder*. Baltimore, MD: Center for Metropolitan Planning and Research, Johns Hopkins University.

Tesce, T. (1994). "Small Agency Bike Patrol." *Law & Order*, 42(7):41-43.

Thurman, Q., P. Quint & A. Giacomazzi (1993). "Program Monitoring & Community Policing: A Process Evaluation of Community Policing in Spokane, Washington." *American Journal of Police*, 12(3):89-114.

Toch, H. (1980). "Mobilizing Police Expertise." In L. Sherman (ed.) *The Police and Violence: The Annals of the American Academy of Political and Social Science*, 452:53-62.

Toch, H. & J. Grant (1991). *Police as Problem Solvers*. New York, NY: Plenum Press.

Tomovich, V. & D. Loree (1989). "In Search of New Directions: Policing in Niagara Region." *Canadian Police College Journal*, 13:29-54.

Tonry, M. & N. Morris (eds.) (1988). *Crime and Justice: A Review of Research*, Volume 8. Chicago, IL: University of Chicago Press.

Trojanowicz, R. (1994). "The Future of Community Policing." In D. Rosenbaum (ed.) *The Challenge of Community Policing: Testing the Promises*. Thousand Oaks, CA: Sage Publications.

Trojanowicz, R. (1992). "Building Support for Community Policing." *Law Enforcement Bulletin*, 61(5):5-13.

Trojanowicz, R. (1989). *Preventing Civil Disturbances: A Community Policing Approach*. East Lansing, MI: Michigan State University, National Center for Community Policing.

Trojanowicz, R. (1984). "Foot Patrol: Some Problem Areas." *Police Chief*, 51:47-49.

Trojanowicz, R. (1983). "An Evaluation of a Neighborhood Foot Patrol Program." *Journal of Police Science and Administration*, 11:410-419.

Trojanowicz, R. (1982). *An Evaluation of the Neighborhood Foot Patrol Program in Flint, Michigan*. East Lansing, MI: Michigan State University, National Neighborhood Foot Patrol Center.

Trojanowicz, R. (1972). "Police-Community Relations." *Criminology*, 9:401-423.

Trojanowicz, R. & D. Banas (1985). *The Impact of Foot Patrol on Black and White Perceptions of Policing*. East Lansing, MI: Michigan State University, National Neighborhood Foot Patrol Center.

Trojanowicz, R. & D. Banas (1985). *Job Satisfaction: A Comparison of Foot Patrol versus Motor Patrol Officers*. East Lansing, MI: Michigan State University, National Neighborhood Foot Patrol Center.

Trojanowicz, R. & D. Banas (1985). *Perceptions of Safety: A Comparison of Foot Patrol versus Motor Patrol Officers*. East Lansing, MI: Michigan State University, National Neighborhood Foot Patrol Center.

Trojanowicz, R. & J. Belknap (1986). *Community Policing: Training Issues*. East Lansing, MI: Michigan State University, National Neighborhood Foot Patrol Center.

Trojanowicz, R. & B. Bucqueroux (1992). *Toward Development of Meaningful and Effective Performance Evaluations*. East Lansing, MI: Michigan State University, National Center for Community Policing.

Trojanowicz, R. & B. Bucqueroux (1991). *Community Policing and the Challenge of Diversity*. East Lansing, MI: Michigan State University, National Center for Community Policing.

Trojanowicz, R. & B. Bucqueroux (1990). *Community Policing: A Contemporary Perspective*. Cincinnati, OH: Anderson Publishing Co.

Trojanowicz, R., B. Bucqueroux, T. McLanus & D. Sinclair (1992). *The Neighborhood Network Center: Part One*. East Lansing, MI: Michigan State University, National Center for Community Policing.

Trojanowicz, R. & D. Carter (1990). "The Changing Face of America." *FBI Law Enforcement Bulletin*, 59:7-12.

Trojanowicz, R. & D. Carter (1988). *The Philosophy and Role of Community Policing*. East Lansing, MI: Michigan State University, National Neighborhood Foot Patrol Center.

Trojanowicz, R., R. Gleason, B. Pollard (Bucqueroux) & D. Sinclair (1987). *Community Polic-ing: Community Input into Police Policy-Making*. East Lansing, MI: Michigan State Uni-versity, National Neighborhood Foot Patrol Center.

Trojanowicz, R. & H. Harden (1985). *The Status of Contemporary Community Policing Pro-grams*. East Lansing, MI: Michigan State University, National Neighborhood Foot Patrol Center.

Trojanowicz, R., V. Kappeler, L. Gaines & B. Bucqueroux (1998). *Community Policing: A Con-temporary Perspective,* Second Edition. Cincinnati, OH: Anderson Publishing Co.

Trojanowicz, R. & M. Moore (1988). *The Meaning of Community in Community Policing*. East Lansing, MI: Michigan State University, National Neighborhood Foot Patrol Center.

Trojanowicz, R. & B. Pollard (Bucqueroux) (1986). *Community Policing: The Line Officer's Perspective*. East Lansing, MI: Michigan State University, National Neighborhood Foot Patrol Center.

Trojanowicz, R., B. Pollard (Bucqueroux), F. Colgan & H. Harden (1986). *Community Policing Programs: A Twenty-Year View*. East Lansing, MI: Michigan State University, National Neighborhood Foot Patrol Center.

Trojanowicz, R., M. Steele & S. Trojanowicz (1986). *Community Policing: A Taxpayer's Per-spective*. East Lansing, MI: Michigan State University, National Neighborhood Foot Patrol Center.

Trojanowicz, R., D. Woods, J. Harpold, R. Reboussin & S. Trojanowicz (1994). *Community Policing: A Survey of Police Departments in the United States*. Washington, DC: Federal Bureau of Investigation/Department of Justice.

Trojanowicz, S. (1992). "Theory of Community Policing." Unpublished thesis for masters of sci-ence degree, Michigan State University, East Lansing, MI.

Uchida, C., B. Frost & S. Annan (1990*). Modern Policing and the Control of Illegal Drugs: Testing New Strategies in Two American Cities*, Summary Report. Washington, DC: National Institute of Justice.

Vera Institute of Justice (1988). *CPOP: Community Policing in Practice*. New York, NY: Vera Institute of Justice.

Vines, M. (1989). *Community and Law Enforcement Against Narcotics: The Dallas Police Department's 1989 Drug Initiative*. Dallas, TX: Dallas Police Department.

Vinzant, J. & L. Crothers (1994). "Street-Level Leadership: The Role of Patrol Officers in Com-munity Policing." *Criminal Justice Review*, 19(2):189-211.

Wadman, R. & S. Bailer (1993). *Community Policing & Crime Prevention in American & Eng-land*. Chicago, IL: University of Illinois.

Wadman, R. & R. Olson (1990). *Community Wellness: A New Theory of Policing*. Washington, DC: Police Executive Research Forum.

Walker, S. (1993). "Does Anyone Remember Team Policing? Lesson of the Team Policing Expe-rience for Community Policing." *American Journal of the Police*, 12(1):33-35.

Walker, S. (1984). "'Broken Windows' and Fractured History: The Use and Misuse of History in Recent Police Patrol Analysis." *Justice Quarterly*, 1:75-90.

Walters, P. (1993). "Community-Oriented Policing: A Blend of Strategies." *FBI Law Enforce-ment Bulletin*, 62(11):20-23.

Wasserman, R. & M. Moore (1988). "Values in Policing." *Perspective in Policing*, 8. Washington, DC: National Institute of Justice.

Weatheritt, M. (1988). "Community Policing: Rhetoric or Reality." In J. Greene & S. Mastrofski (eds.) *Community Policing: Rhetoric or Reality*. New York, NY: Praeger.

Weatheritt, M. (1987). "Community Policing Now." In P. Wilmott (ed.) *Policing & the Community*. London, England: Policy Studies Institute.

Weatheritt, M. (1983). "Community Policing: Does It Work & How Do We Know?" In T. Bennett (ed.) *The Future of Policing*, Cropwood Conference Series Number 15, Cambridge, England: Institute of Criminology.

Webber, A. (1991). "Crime and Management: An Interview with New York City Police Commissioner Lee P. Brown." *Harvard Business Review*, 69:111-126.

Webster, B. & E. Connors (1993). "Police Methods for Identifying Community Problems." *American Journal of Police*. 12(1):75-101.

Weick, K. (1984). "Small Wins: Redefining the Scale of Social Problems." *American Psychologist*, 39:40-49.

Weisborn, M., H. Lamb & A. Drexler (1974). *Improving Police Department Management Through Problem-Solving Task Forces: A Case Study in Organization Development*. Reading, MA: Addison-Wesly.

Weisburd, D. & J. McElroy (1988). "Enacting the CPO Role: Findings from the New York City Pilot Program in Community Policing." In J. Greene & S. Mastrofski (eds.) *Community Policing: Rhetoric or Reality*. New York, NY: Praeger.

Weisburd, D., J. McElroy & P. Hardyman (1988). "Challenges to Supervision in Community Policing: Observations on a Pilot Project." *American Journal of Police*, 7:29-59.

Weisburd, D., C. Uchida & L. Green (1993). *Police Innovation & Control of the Police: Problems of Law, Order & Community.* New York, NY: Springer-Verlag.

Weisel, D. (1990). "Playing the Home Field: A Problem-Oriented Approach to Drug Control." *American Journal of Police*, 9:75-95.

Weisel, D. (1990). *Tackling Drug Problems in Public Housing: A Guide for Police.* Washington, DC: Police Executive Research Forum.

Weisel, D. & J. Eck (1994). "Toward a Practical Approach to Organizational Change: Community Policing Initiatives in Six Cities." In D. Rosenbaum *The Challenge of Community Policing: Testing the Promises* (Chapter 3). Thousand Oaks, CA: Sage Publications.

Weston, J. (1993). "Community Policing: An Approach to Youth Gangs in a Medium-Sized City." *Police Chief*, 60(8):80-84.

Weston, J. (1991). "Community Policing: An Approach to Traffic Management." *Law and Order*, 39:32-36.

Williams, H. & A. Pate (1987). "Returning to First Principles: Reducing the Fear of Crime in Newark." *Crime & Delinquency*, 33:53-70.

Williams, J. & R. Sloan (1990). *Turning Concept into Practice: The Aurora, Colorado Story.* East Lansing, MI: Michigan State University, National Center for Community Policing.

Wilson, D. & S. Bennett (1994). "Officer's Response to Community Policing: Variations on a Theme." *Crime & Delinquency*, 33:53-70.

Wilson, J. (1983). *Thinking About Crime*. New York, NY: Basic Books.

Wilson, J. & G. Kelling (1989, February). "Making Neighborhoods Safe." *Atlantic Monthly*, pp. 46-52.

Wilson, J. & G. Kelling (1982, March). "Broken Windows." *Atlantic Monthly*, pp. 29-38.

Winkel, F. (1988). "The Police and Reducing Fear of Crime: A Comparison of the Crime-Centered and the Quality of Life Approaches." *Police Studies*, 11:183-189.

Witte, J., L. Travis III & R. Langworthy (1990). "Participatory Management in Law Enforcement: Police Officer, Supervisor and Administrator Perceptions." *American Journal of Police*, 9:1-24.

Wolford, J. (1994). "Conflict & Controversy. Can the Chief Fill the Void?" *Police Chief*, 61(1):52, 54.

Woy, P. (1994). "Bicycles The Perfect Bridge Between Foot & Car Patrol." *Law & Order*, 42(3):99-101.

Wycoff, M. (1988). "The Benefits of Community Policing: Evidence and Conjecture." In J. Greene & S. Mastrofski (eds.) *Community Policing: Rhetoric or Reality*. New York, NY: Praeger.

Wycoff, M. & P. Manning (1983). "The Police and Crime Control." In G. Whitaker & C. Phillips (eds.) *Evaluating Performance of Criminal Justice Agencies*, pp. 15-32. Beverly Hills, CA: Sage Publications.

Wycoff, M. & W. Skogan (1994). "The Effect of a Community Policing Management Style on Officers' Attitudes." *Crime & Delinquency*, 40(3):371-383.

Yin, R. (1986). "Community Crime Prevention: A Synthesis of Eleven Evaluations." In D. Rosenbaum (ed.) *Community Crime Prevention: Does it Work?* Beverly Hills, CA: Sage Publications.

Young, J. (1991). "Left Realism and the Priorities of Crime Control." In K. Stenson & D. Cowell (eds.) *The Politics of Crime Control*, pp. 146-160. London, UK: Sage Publications.

Zhao, J. (1996). *Why Police Organizations Change: A Study of Community-Oriented Policing*. Washington, DC: Police Executive Research Forum.

Zhao, J. & Q. Thurman (1996). *The Nature of Community Policing Innovation: DO the Ends Justify the Means?* Washington, DC: Police Executive Research Forum.

Zhao, J., Q. Thurman & N. Lovirch (1995). "Community-Oriented Policing Across the U.S.: Facilitators & Impediments to Implementation." *American Journal of Police*, (1):11-28.

Ziembo-Vogl, J. & D. Woods (1996). "Defining Community Policing: Practice Versus Paradigm." *Police Studies*, 19(3):33-50.